Grade 1.2

Scott Foresman
Practice Book

PEARSON

Scott Foresman

Editorial Offices: Glenview, Illinois • Parsippany, New Jersey • New York, New York
Sales Offices: Needham, Massachusetts • Duluth, Georgia • Glenview, Illinois
Coppell, Texas • Sacramento, California • Mesa, Arizona

ISBN: 0-328-14516-5

7 8 9 10 V011 16 15 14 13 12 11 10 09 08 07

Contents

Unit 3
Changes

Unit 4
Treasures

© Pearson Education 1

Contents

Unit 5
Great Ideas

Practice Book

Family Times

You are your child's first and best teacher!

This week we're

Reading An Egg Is an Egg

An Egg Is an Egg
by Nicki Weiss
When is an egg not an egg?

Talking About How we change as we grow

Learning About Vowel Sounds of *y*
Long Vowels (CV)
Compare and Contrast

Here are ways to help your child practice skills while having fun!

Day 1

Write *baby, busy, cry, dry, family, fly, fry, happy, lucky, pony, silly, sly, try, why.* Take turns reading a word with your child. If the *y* sounds like long *i*, circle the word with blue. If the *y* sounds like long *e*, circle the word with red.

Day 2

Write each letter on a card: *b, e, g, h, i, m, n, o, s, w.* Together match a consonant to a vowel to make a two-letter word. Words include: *be, me, hi, go, no, so, we, he.*

Day 3

Write these words: *always, become, day, everything, nothing, stays, things.* Give clues for each word. Have your child guess the answer, point to the word, and read it.

Day 4

Write each spelling word on a card: *my, by, try, any, body, fly, cry, lucky, silly, puppy.* Have your child sort the words by ending sound long *e* or long *i*. Take turns reading the words.

Day 5

This week your child is learning to look for similarities and differences in stories. As you read together, ask your child how certain things are the same or different.

Here Fishy, Fishy

Materials paper, marker, scissors, 10 paper clips, 24-inch piece of string, small magnet, ruler or wooden spoon

Game Directions

1. Prepare a set of 12 paper fish as shown. Then make two fish bowl shapes. On one write "y as long i." On the other bowl write "y as long e."

2. Tie one end of the string to the magnet and the other end to a ruler or wooden spoon.

3. Put a paper clip on each fish. Scatter the fish on the floor and take turns catching them with the magnet "bait."

4. When a player catches a fish, the player says the word, spells it, and then puts the fish by the proper fish bowl. Play continues until all the fish are caught.

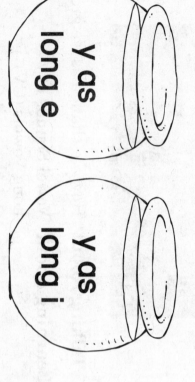

y as long e

y as long i

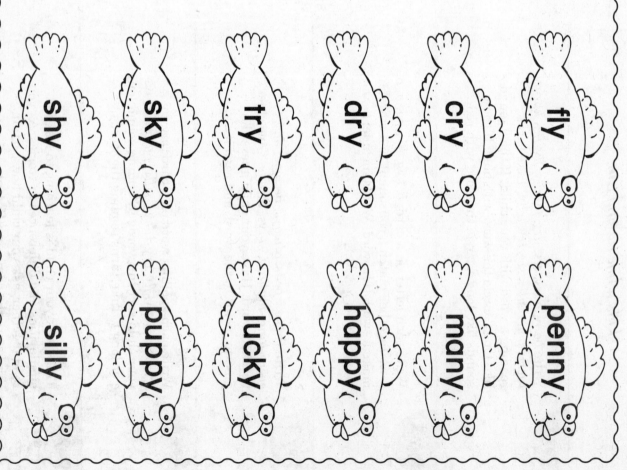

shy

sky

try

dry

cry

fly

silly

puppy

lucky

happy

many

penny

© Pearson Education 1

Name _____

 fr**y**

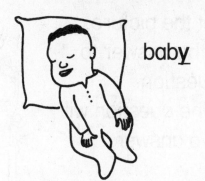 bab**y**

Circle the word for each picture.

1.	2.	3.	4.
puppy put	flop fly	lock lucky	bunny ball

5.	6.	7.	8.
crib cry	sit city	sky skate	had happy

Find the word that has the same **y** sound as
Mark the ⬭ to show your answer.

9. ⬭ mommy
⬭ messy
⬭ my

10. ⬭ tummy
⬭ try
⬭ twenty

School + Home

Home Activity Your child practiced reading words with the vowel sounds of *y* heard in *fry* or *baby*. Work with your child to put the above answers into two word lists—one of words in which *y* represents the long *e* sound (*baby*) and one in which it represents the long *i* sound (*fry*).

© Pearson Education 1

Name _____

Look at the picture.
Circle the answer to
each question.
Hint: One question will
have two answers.

1. Who has a dress?   Kate   Amy

2. Who has pants?   Kate   Amy

3. Who has a cat?   Kate   Amy

4. Who has no pet?   Kate   Amy

5. Who has a pen?   Kate   Amy

6. **Draw** two cats that are the same.

7. **Draw** two cats that are different.

Home Activity Your child identified the ways in which two characters were alike and different. Have your child describe two of his or her relatives. Have your child tell how they are alike and different.

4 Comprehension Compare and Contrast   **Practice Book Unit 3**

Name _____

Circle a word to finish each sentence.
Write it on the line.

n**o**

He   Hi

_____

- - - - - - - - - - - - - - - - - - -

1. "_____", Luke said.

Hi   He

_____

- - - - - - - - - - - - - - - - - - -

2. _____ is little.

No   Nod

_____

- - - - - - - - - - - - - - - - - - -

3. _____ one can see him.

so   see

_____

- - - - - - - - - - - - - - - - - - -

4. She is _____ big.

bed   be

_____

- -

5. He will grow to _____ big too.

School + Home

Home Activity Your child practiced reading words with the long vowel pattern heard in *me*, *hi*, and *go*. Work with your child to make a list of words with the long *e* sound spelled *e* and the long *o* sound spelled *o*.

Name _____

Pick a word from the box to complete each sentence.
Write it on the line.

| always becomes day everything |
| nothing stays things |

_____
- -
1. Jazzy likes to play all _____ .

_____
- -
2. _____ can stop him!

_____
- -
3. He gets into _____ .

_____
- -
4. He _____ makes a mess.

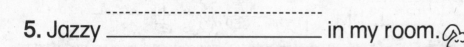

_____
- -
5. Jazzy _____ in my room.

_____
- -
6. He hides _____ under the bed.

_____
- -
7. He rests when he _____ sleepy.

Home Activity This week your child learned to read the words *always, becomes, day, everything, nothing, stays,* and *things*. Use paper bag puppets to act out a scene using these new words.

6 High-Frequency Words

Practice Book Unit 3

Name _____

Write a word from the box to finish each sentence.
Hint: You will not use one word.

| always becomes day everything |
| grew nothing stays things |

_____

1. Dave _____ plays in the sand.

_____

2. The boy makes a tower every _____ .

_____

3. _____ will stop him.

_____

4. He also looks for _____ in the sand.

_____

5. At sunset, day _____ night.

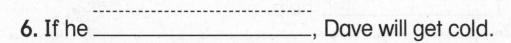

_____

6. If he _____, Dave will get cold.

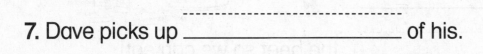

_____

7. Dave picks up _____ of his.

 Home Activity This week your child learned to read the words *always, becomes, boy, day, everything, grew, night, nothing, stays, sunset, things,* and *tower.* Help your child make up a song using some of these words. Help your child to write down the song and perform it for other family members.

Name _____

Circle a word to finish each sentence.
Write it on the line.

tr<u>ee</u>

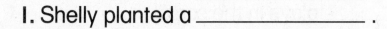

seed   sad

_____

- - - - - - - - - - - - - - - - - - -

1. Shelly planted a _____ .

weds   weeds

_____

- - - - - - - - - - - - - - - - - - -

2. Shelly and Lee got the _____ out.

he   hi

_____

- - - - - - - - - - - - - - - - - - -

3. "I see a big beet!" _____ said.

nod   need

_____

- - - - - - - - - - - - - - - - - - -

4. Lee said, "I _____ help."

peel   pal

_____

- - - - - - - - - - - - - - - - - - -

5. Mom will _____ the beet so we can eat!

School + Home

Home Activity Your child practiced reading words with long *e* as heard in *me* and *bee*. Work with your child to make a list of words that rhyme with *deep* and a list that rhymes with *me*.

Name _____

Pick letters from the box to finish each word.
Write the letters on the lines.

bu**tt**on

dd	ll	pp	sk

_____
1. The man rakes the fa _____ en leaves.

_____
2. Plants are in a ba _____ et.

_____
3. A bee gets the po _____ en.

_____
4. A kitten is hi _____ en.

_____
5. What will ha _____ en when he wants the plants?

Home Activity Your child completed words with two syllables that have two consonants in the middle. Name some plants and flowers that grow in your community. Ask your child to identify the middle consonant sounds in the words.

© Pearson Education 1

Practice Book Unit 3

Phonics Syllables VCCV Review

9

Name _____

A B C D E F G H I J K L M N O P Q R S T U V W X Y Z

Write the words in each box in ABC order.

things	always
flower	branch

nothing	good
small	chick

1. _____

2. _____

3. _____

4. _____

5. _____

6. _____

7. _____

8. _____

Circle the correct answer about a glossary page.

9. Between which two guide words would you look for the word **some**?

        saw / tag   day / eat   mat / nut

10. Between which two guide words would you look for the word **block**?

        cat / bag   tell / up   baby / can

Home Activity Your child put words in alphabetical order and learned how to use guide words. Write the names of family members on slips of paper. Each name should begin with a different letter. Ask your child to put the names in ABC order.

© Pearson Education 1

Family Times

You are your child's first and best teacher!

This week we're

Reading Ruby in Her Own Time

Ruby in
Her Own
Time

by Jonathan Emmett

Illustrated by:
Rebecca Harry

*What will Ruby
learn as she grows?*

Talking About What we learn as we
grow and change

Learning About Final *ng, nk*
Compound Words
Plot

---

*Here are ways to help your child practice
skills while having fun!*

Day 1

Write each word on a card: *king, thing, wing,
sing, kink, think, wink, sink, sank, tank, bank,
thank.* Have your child read the words.

Day 2

Write each compound word: *someone,
somebody, softball, anybody, anyway, dugout,
anyone.* Cut the words apart between the two
small words. Mix the cards and play a
matching game together.

Day 3

Write *any, enough, ever, every, own, sure, were.*
Have your child dictate a sentence for each word.

Day 4

Write each spelling word: *bring, trunk, pink, bank,
sang, wing, rink, blank, rang, sunk.* Together, trace
the letters as you read the words.

Day 5

Your child is learning to recognize the
beginning, middle, and end of a story. As you
read together, stop to discuss the events at the
beginning, middle, and end of the story.

Compound Treasures

Materials paper, marker, scissors, paper clip, pencil, 1 button per player

Game Directions

1. Make a simple spinner as shown.
2. Players place buttons on Start, take turns spinning, and move the number of spaces shown. Pick one player to be the recorder.
3. Each player must use the word shown on the space with a word from the list below to make a compound word. The recorder writes the word on lined paper. Play continues until all players have reached End.
4. All players then read the list of words they made together.

house	top	ball
side	cake	cone	end
hive	mother	one	pack
hill	time	cup	self

1	2
3	4

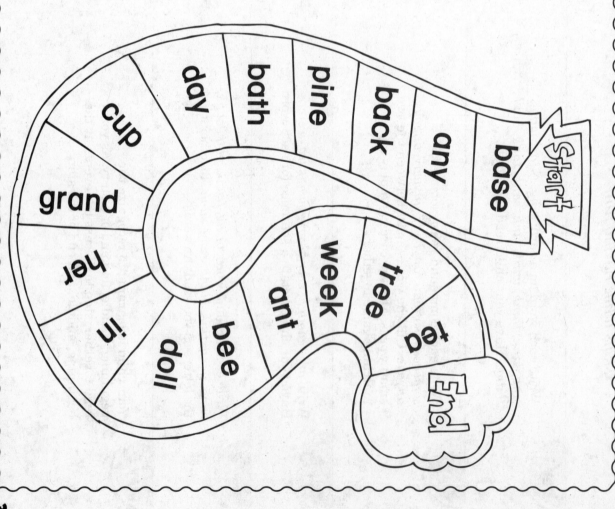

© Pearson Education 1

Name _____

 ri**ng**

 ba**nk**

Circle the word for each picture.

1. 	2. 	3. 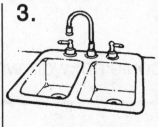	4. 
sink sing	skunk skate	sink side	kink king

5. 	6. 	7. 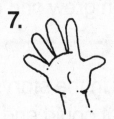	8. 
wink wing	trunk truck	hand hang	swim swing

Find the word that has the same ending sound as  .
Mark the ⟞ to show your answer.

9. ⟞ sand
   ⟞ sang
   ⟞ sank

10. ⟞ thin
    ⟞ think
    ⟞ thing

 Home Activity Your child read words that end with *ng* and *nk*. Say one of the words with *ng* or *nk* on this page and ask your child to say a word that rhymes with it. Then have your child say a word for you to rhyme.

Name _____

Read the sentences in the story.
Number the sentences from 1 to 3 to show what happens first, next and last.

_____

1. _____ Now he is six, and he can jump and run fast.

_____

2. _____ Ben could not walk when he was one.

_____

3. _____ Then Ben grew and could walk.

Read the sentences in the story.
Write a sentence that could end the story.

Beth was small.
Beth grew up.

_____

4. _____

_____

_____

_____

Home Activity Your child learned how to identify the beginning, middle, and end of a story. As you read stories with your child, have your child tell you what parts of the story are important and the order in which they happened.

Name _____

Pick a word from the box to finish each compound word.
Write it on the line.
Draw a line to the picture it matches.

ball   cakes   pole   set

sidewalk

1. pan _____

5.

2. sun _____

6.

3. flag _____

7.

4. base _____

8.

Find the compound word.
Mark the ⬭ to show your answer.

9. ⬭ sandy
⬭ sandman
⬭ sanding

10. ⬭ napkin
⬭ happen
⬭ dishpan

Home Activity Your child read compound words—words formed by joining two or more other words. Walk
around your house with your child and find things you see that are compound words *(toothbrush, hairbrush,
bathtub).* Say each word and have your child identify the two words used to make the compound word.

Name _____

Write a word from the box to finish each sentence.

| any enough ever every own sure were |

1. Do we have ☐☐☐☐☐ food?

2. Yes, I am ☐☐☐☐ we do.

3. Is ☐☐☐☐ place set?

4. Yes, they ☐☐☐☐ set last night.

5. Do you need ☐☐☐ flowers?

6. No, I have my ☐☐☐ .

7. This will be the best day ☐☐☐☐ !

Home Activity This week your child learned to read the words *any, enough, ever, every, own, sure,* and *were*. Help your child make up a short story using some of these words. Then help your child to write down the sentences and draw a picture to go with his or her story.

Name _____

Pick a word from the box to finish each sentence.
Write the missing word part on the line.

┌─────────────────────┐
│   any   every   │
└─────────────────────┘

_____
- - - - - - - - - - - - - - - - -
1. Flowers are _____ where!

_____
- - - - - - - - - - - - - - - -
2. Is there _____ one you like best?

Pick a word from the box to finish each sentence.
Write the word on the line.

┌──────────────────────────────┐
│ enough   ever   own   │
│   sure   were   │
└──────────────────────────────┘

_____
- - - - - - - - - - - - - - - -
3. My father has his _____ precious dog.

_____
- - - - - - - - - - - - - - - -
4. Are you _____ the bird ever flew?

_____
- - - - - - - - - - - - - - - -
5. His feathers _____ always pretty!

_____
- - - - - - - - - - - - - - - -
6. Will you _____ get a cat?

_____
- - - - - - - - - - - - - - - -
7. My mother says two pets are _____ .

Home Activity This week your child learned to read the words *any, beautiful, enough, ever, every, father, feathers, flew, mother, own, precious, sure,* and *were.* Help your child make up a short story using some of these words. Help your child to write down the sentences and draw a picture to go with his or her story.

Name _____

Write a word from the box to match each picture.
Circle the word if it ends like **baby**.
Underline the word if it ends like **cry**.

| bunny | city | fly |
| fry | puppy | silly |

The baby will <u>cry</u>.

1.

_____

2.

_____

3.

_____

4.

_____

5.

_____

6.

_____

Draw a picture of each word.

7. candy

8. sky

Home Activity Your child reviewed reading and writing words with the vowel sounds of *y* heard in *baby* or *cry*. Have your child list words that rhyme with *my*. Then list words that rhyme with *berry*.

Name _____

Pick a word from the box to finish each sentence.
Write it on the line.
Remember to begin a sentence with a capital letter.

be	go	hi	she	so

m<u>e</u>

_____
- - - - - - - - - - - - - - -
1. _____ is five.

_____
- - - - - - - - - - - - - - -
2. She will _____ six one day.

_____
- - - - - - - - - - - - - - -
3. She will _____ into a tent.

_____
- - - - - - - - - - - - - - -
4. That man is _____ funny.

_____
- - - - - - - - - - - - - - -
5. He said _____ to me.

School + Home **Home Activity** Your child reviewed reading words with the long vowel pattern heard in *me*, *hi*, and *go*. Read one of the words from the box and have your child use it in a new sentence.

Practice Book Unit 3   **Phonics** Long Vowels (CV) Review **19**

Name _____

Find these words in the Glossary of your student book.
Draw a picture to show what each word means.

1. feather

2. mother

3. night

4. rain

5. father

6. flew

Home Activity Your child learned how to use a glossary to look up the meaning of words. Find a glossary in a book at home or at the library and work with your child to look up other words.

© Pearson Education 1

Family Times

You are your child's first and best teacher!

Here are ways to help your child practice skills while having fun!

This week we're

Reading Jan's New Home

Jan's New Home
by Angela Shelf Medearis
illustrated by Don Tate

What will change
when Jan moves
to a new home?

Talking About Why changes are exciting

Learning About Ending -es; Plural -es
r-Controlled or, ore
Theme

Day 1

Write these words in a list: *glass, bus, mix, fix, dish, brush, patch, pitch.* Read aloud each word to your child. Then say the same word, but add *-es* to the end. Have your child write and read the new words.

Day 2

Write the following word parts on cards: *-ore, -ort,* and *-orn.* Make letter cards for: *c, t, w, s, sh.* Take turns making words. (*core, corn, tore, torn, wore, worn, sore, sort, shore, short*)

Day 3

Write the following words in a list: *away, car, friends, house, our, school, very.* Take turns picking a word and making up a riddle for the other player to guess the word.

Day 4

Write the spelling words on cards: *bus, buses, fix, fixes, class, classes, wish, wishes, kiss, kisses.* Take turns choosing a card and writing a sentence for the word.

Day 5

This week your child is learning about the theme, or the big idea, in a story. As you read together this week, stop and discuss the big idea of the story.

More, More, More!

Materials paper circle, paper clip, pencils, 1 button per player.

Game Directions

1. Make a simple spinner as shown.

2. Take turns spinning the spinner and moving the correct number of spaces. When the player lands on a word, he or she must read the word correctly to stay on that space. If the player does not do so, he or she must move back one space.

3. The first player to reach the pet store wins!

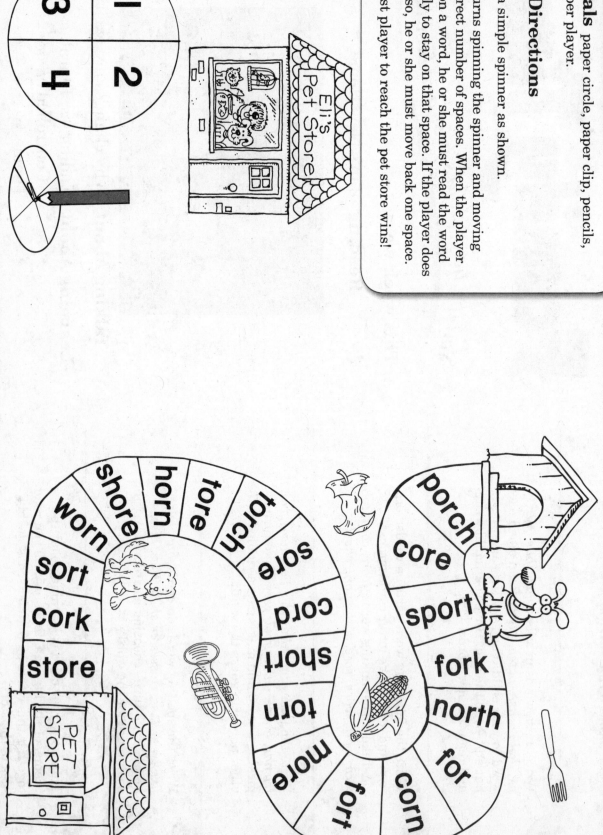

Name _____

Greg fix**es** the benches.

Add the ending.
Write the new word on the line.

Word	Ending	New Word
1. mix	+ -es	_____
2. brush	+ -es	_____
3. glass	+ -es	_____
4. catch	+ -es	_____
5. dress	+ -es	_____
6. bus	+ -es	_____
7. dish	+ -es	_____
8. fox	+ -es	_____
9. nut	+ -s	_____
10. patch	+ -es	_____

© Pearson Education 1

School + Home

Home Activity Your child added -es to verbs and nouns. Have your child use each new word in a sentence.

Name _____

Read the story.
Draw a picture of the big idea of the story.

Max and Sam

Max had a new puppy.
Sam was sad. He had no pet.
Max said, "Play with us!"
Max and Sam played with
the puppy. Sam was happy.
Max was happy too.

1.

---

2. Circle the big idea of the story.

People like animals.

People feel happy when they do a good thing.

Think about the last time you did a good thing for a pal.
Draw a picture that shows what you did.

3.

© Pearson Education 1

Home Activity Your child learned about the theme, or the big idea, in a story. Tell your child a story about a childhood event of yours. Then discuss the big idea of the story. Invite your child to tell you about a similar experience of his or hers.

Name _____

Circle the word for each picture.

 stormt... st<u>or</u>m

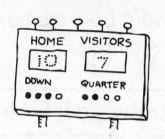 sc<u>ore</u>

1.

fork   flick

2.

hen   horn

3.

core   conk

4.

store   stock

5.

con   corn

6.

shorts   shots

7.

port   pot

8.

thorn   tone

Find the word that has the same middle sound as  .
Mark the ⬭ to show your answer.

9. ⬭ porch
    ⬭ poke
    ⬭ pole

10. ⬭ such
    ⬭ shut
    ⬭ shore

 School + Home **Home Activity** Your child read words with *or* as in *storm* and *ore* as in *score*. Help your child make up a story using words with this vowel sound, such as *snore*, *horn*, *popcorn*, and *short*. Then have your child illustrate his or her story.

Name _____

Pick a word from the box to complete each sentence.
Write it on the line.

> away   car   friends   house   our   school   very

_____
1. This is our new _____ .

_____
2. It is by my _____ .

_____
3. It is _____ nice.

_____
4. We go with our _____ .

_____
5. They come in a _____ .

_____
6. My mom will walk _____ . I will stay.

_____
7. _____ teacher is inside.

Home Activity This week your child learned to read the words *away, car, friends, house, our, school,* and *very.* Use sock puppets to act out a new story using the words. Help your child write down the story you create.

© Pearson Education 1

Name _____

Pick a word from the box to finish each sentence.
Write the words in the puzzles.

away	car	friends	house	our	school	very

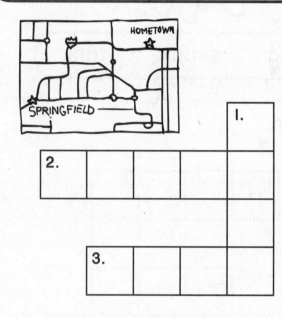

1. We have to move _____ far from here.

2. Our _____ has a big window in back.

3. I am sad to move _____ .

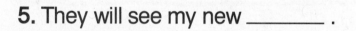

4. My _____ will come to see me.

5. They will see my new _____ .

6. They will come in their _____ .

7. We will play with _____ toys.

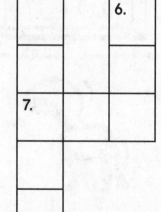

School + Home **Home Activity** This week your child learned to read the words *away, car, friends, house, move, our, school, toys, very,* and *window.* Take turns reading each word in the box and using it in a sentence.

© Pearson Education 1

Name _____

Pick a word from the box to match each clue.
Write the words in the puzzles.

 ri**ng**    ba**nk**

| bank | fang | king | skunk | tank |

1.

2.

3.

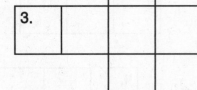

4.

5.

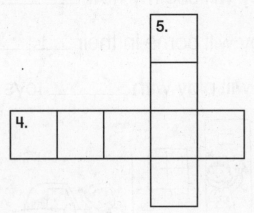

Home Activity Your child solved two puzzles with words that end with *ng* and *nk*. Have your child use each word in a sentence.

28 **Phonics** Word Final *ng, nk* Review   **Practice Book Unit 3**

© Pearson Education 1

Name _____

Circle the compound word in each sentence.

 greenhouse

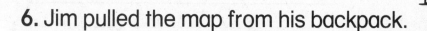

1. This weekend Jim will be in his new house.

2. He will miss his classmates.

3. His mom made homemade candy.

4. Ms. Hill made popcorn.

5. Jim gave a cupcake to Ms. Hill.

6. Jim pulled the map from his backpack.

7. He will live by the shoreline.

8. Jim will take his bulldog with him.

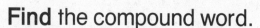

Find the compound word.

Mark the ⬭ to show your answer.

9. ⬭ shortstop
   ⬭ shorten
   ⬭ shore

10. ⬭ weedy
    ⬭ weeks
    ⬭ weekend

Home Activity Your child reviewed compound words—words formed by joining two or more words. Write words such as *out, side, in, any, thing, base, ball, some, where,* and *one* on separate slips of paper. Have your child form compound words.

Name _____

Look at the map.
Write the answer to each question.

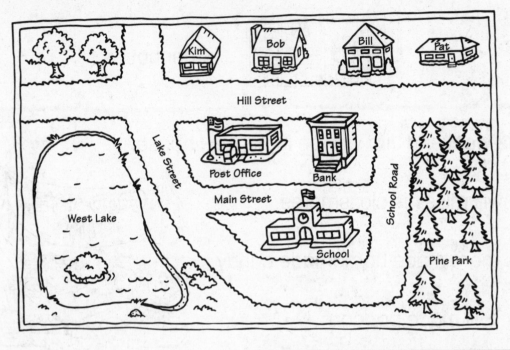

_____
1. What street does Bill live on? _____
_____

2. What street is the bank on? _____

3. Who lives closer to West Lake—Kim or Bob?

_____
_____
_____

4. Which street would Pat take to get to school quickly?

_____
_____

© Pearson Education 1

Home Activity Your child read a map and answered questions about it. Look at a map of your town with your child. Go over the different symbols and explain what they mean. Then point out two places and ask your child to show you how to get from one place to the other.

Family Times

You are your child's first and best teacher!

This week we're

Reading Frog and Toad Together

Frog and Toad
Together

by Arnold Lobel

The Garden

What do seeds need to grow?

Talking About Changes that happen in a garden

Learning About Inflected Endings -ed, -ing
r-Controlled ar
Plot

Here are ways to help your child practice skills while having fun!

Day 1

Write *dipped, dipping, jabbed, jabbing, kicked, kicking*. Have your child read the words and circle the base words.

Day 2

Write the following words on cards: *car, far, jar, barn, yarn, yard, hard, smart*. Have your child read aloud each word.

Day 3

Write the following words in a list: *afraid, again, few, how, read, soon*. Make up a sentence using each word, but say "blank" instead of the word. Have your child tell the missing word.

Day 4

Write each spelling word on a card: *ask, asked, plan, planned, help, helped, jog, jogged, call, called*. Together, sort the words by *happening now* and *happened then*.

Day 5

This week your child is learning to recognize the beginning, middle, and end of a story. After reading a story together, write a sentence that tells the beginning, the middle, and the end. Have your child number them in the correct order.

Arrrrrgh, Matey!

Materials index cards, scissors, marker, real coin

Game Directions

1. Cut circles from index cards and label them like the ones on page 3.

2. Shuffle the pieces and place them face down on the table.

3. Each player flips a coin. If it lands heads up, the player takes two pieces. If it lands tails up, the player takes one piece.

4. Each player reads aloud the word on the piece. Then he or she must think of a new word that could be formed by changing the letters *ar* to *or* or *ore* to make a new word. For example, *tar* could be changed to *tore*. If the player can think of a new word, he or she can keep the treasure piece.

5. Play then passes to the next person. Play continues until all the pieces have been collected.

Answers: core, form, bore, score, pork, card, for, born, pod, turn, store

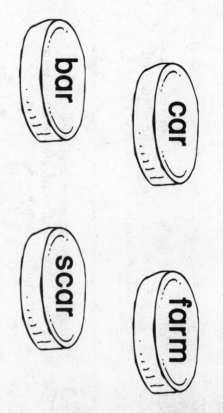

car farm
bar scar
park card
far barn
part star

Name _____

Dan is mop**ping** up the mess.
The mess is mop**ped** up.

Add -ed and **-ing** to each word.
Write the new words on the line.

	Add -ed	**Add -ing**
1. nap		
2. pat		
3. nod		
4. jog		
5. wag		
6. stop		
7. pet		
8. drop		
9. clap		
10. plan		

Home Activity Your child practiced writing words that end in *-ed* and *-ing*. Together with your child make up a story using the words above.

Name _____

Read the sentences in the story.
Number them from 1 to 3 to show the right order.

_____

1. _____ Little green shoots came up.

_____

2. _____ The shoots turned into beautiful flowers.

_____

3. _____ Kate planted many seeds.

Read the sentence that begins the story.
Write a sentence that could be in the middle of the story.
Write a sentence that could end the story.

This is a small plant.

_____

4. _____

_____

5. _____

 School + Home **Home Activity** Your child learned how to identify the beginning, middle, and end of a story. As you discuss the story with your child, have your child tell you what parts of the story were important to him or her and the order in which events happened.

Name _____

Circle the word for each picture.

f**ar**m

1.

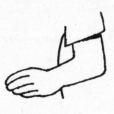

arm   am

2.

band   barn

3.

core   car

4.

far   jam

5.

duck   dark

6.

party   patty

7.

cart   cork

8.

cord   card

Find the word that rhymes with ⭐ .
Mark the ⬭ to show your answer.

---

9. ⬭ form
   ⬭ far
   ⬭ for

10. ⬭ tar
    ⬭ torn
    ⬭ trap

School + Home

Home Activity Your child read words with *ar* as in *farm*. Help your child make up a story about a car trip. Encourage your child to use words with *ar* that have the same vowel sound as *car*.

Name _____

Circle a word to finish each sentence.
Write it on the line.

how   few

_____

- - - - - - - - - - - - - - - - - - -

1. We have a _____ to take back.

afraid   read

_____

- - - - - - - - - - - - - - - -

2. We _____ them all and came for new ones.

again   few

_____

- - - - - - - - - - - - - - - - - - - -

3. Can we get some _____ ?

soon   how

_____

- - - - - - - - - - - - - - - - - -

4. We can read _____ to plant flowers.

afraid   few

_____

- - - - - - - - - - - - - - - - - -

5. I am _____ this is not the best one.

afraid   soon

_____

- - - - - - - - - - - - - - - - - -

6. My mom will be here _____ .

School + Home

Home Activity This week your child learned to read the words *afraid, again, few, how, read,* and *soon.* Make some flash cards and have your child practice reading the words.

Name _____

Pick a word from the box to finish each sentence.
Write it on the line.

| afraid | again | few | how | read | soon |

_____
----

1. There were a _____ drops of rain
   on the ground, so Danny went in.

_____
----

2. Then it started to rain _____ , and the rain came
   down hard.

_____
----

3. "Do not be _____ of the rain,"
   said his mom as she patted his head.

_____
----

4. Mom said, "It will end _____ ."

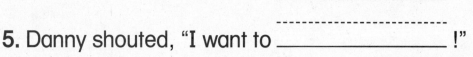

_____
----

5. Danny shouted, "I want to _____ !"

6. Mom said, "Stop shouting. Then we can read
   _____

   _____ the rain helps the garden!"

Home Activity This week your child learned to read the words *afraid, again, few, ground, head, how, rain, read, shouted, shouting,* and *soon.* Write the words in a list. Have your child point to a word, read it, and then make up a sentence using the word. Then he or she can draw a picture of some of the sentences.

© Pearson Education 1

Name _____

Add -s or **-es** to each verb.
Write the new verb on the line.

1. fix

_____

- - - - - - - - - - - - - - - - - -

_____

2. kiss

_____

- - - - - - - - - - - - - - - - - -

_____

3. run

_____

- - - - - - - - - - - - - - - - - -

_____

4. wish

_____

- - - - - - - - - - - - - - - - - -

_____

5. help

_____

- - - - - - - - - - - - - - - - - -

_____

6. catch

_____

- - - - - - - - - - - - - - - - - -

_____

Add -es to each word.
Write the new word on the line.
Draw a picture of the word.

7. box

_____

- - - - - - - - - - - - - - - - - -

_____

8.

9. glass

_____

- - - - - - - - - - - - - - - - - -

_____

10.

Home Activity Your child added *-s* and *-es* to verbs and nouns. Look through a catalog or magazine with your child. Take turns naming pictures that show more than one item. Then have your child use the plural word in a sentence.

Name _____

Circle a word to finish each sentence.
Write it on the line.

 h**or**n

born   bond

_____

- -

I. Tadpoles were _____ .

most   more

_____

- -

2. I see _____ than three!

form   fond

_____

- -

3. It will _____ legs.

store   storm

_____

- -

4. Then a _____ came. I saw a head pop out.

shot   shore

_____

- -

5. The frog swam to _____ .

 School + Home   **Home Activity** Your child reviewed words with *or* that have the sound heard in *horn*. Work with your child to make a list of words that rhyme with *horn* and *more*.

© Pearson Education 1

Name _____

Look at the diagram.
Follow the directions.

Rose

flower

leaves

bud

leaves

thorn

stem

1. **Circle** two buds.

2. **Draw** an X on two leaves.

3. **Underline** the title.

4. **Write** the part of the plant that
   holds up the flower.
   _____
   -
   _____

5. **Number** the pictures from 1 to 3 to show the order in which
   they happened.

_____
- - - - - - - - - - - -
_____

_____
- - - - - - - - - - - -
_____

_____
- - - - - - - - - - - -
_____

© Pearson Education 1

School + Home **Home Activity** Your child learned to read a labeled diagram. As you interact with your child this week, point
out any simple diagrams you see and discuss the information they provide with your child.

Family Times

You are your child's first and best teacher!

This week we're

Reading I'm a Caterpillar

Talking About Changes we can observe in nature

Learning About *r*-Controlled *er, ir, ur*
Contractions *'s, 've, 're*
Draw Conclusions

Here are ways to help your child practice skills while having fun!

Day 1

Write these words on cards and turn them face down: *perch, serve, dirt, third, curb, surf*. Take turns picking a card and offering clues so the other person can guess the word. Then have your child read the words.

Day 2

Write these phrases: *she is, they have, we are, he is, you have, you are, we have*. Take turns writing the correct contraction for each phrase.

Day 3

Write the following words in a list: *done, know, push, visit, wait*. Have your child write sentences that use at least one list word in each.

Day 4

Write each spelling word on a card: *her, first, bird, girl, burn, were, shirt, fur, hurt, sir*. Sort the words by rules of your child's choice.

Day 5

This week your child is learning to draw conclusions about the story based on the text and what your child already knows. As you read together, ask for conclusions about the events, place, or characters.

Turn into a Butterfly

Materials crayons, paper, scissors, tape

Game Directions

1. Together, read the words in the caterpillar.
2. Color the *ur* words green. Color the *or* words orange. Color the *er* words yellow. Color the *ir* words yellow.
3. Make butterfly wings. Ask your child to write a new *ur, ir* or *er* word on each wing. Attach the wings to the caterpillar.

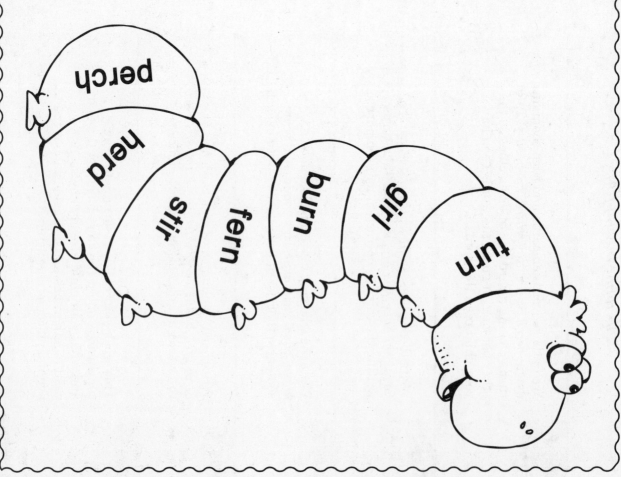

perch

herd

stir

fern

burn

girl

turn

Name _____

h**er**   b**ir**d   s**ur**f

Circle the word for each picture.

1. 	**2.** 	**3.** 	**4.** 
short shirt	clerk click	curl chill	barn burn

5. 	**6.** 	**7.** 	**8.** 
fern fan	skirt skit	fist first	stir store

Find the word that has the same vowel sound as .
Mark the ⬭ to show your answer.

9. ⬭ hard
   ⬭ hut
   ⬭ hurt

10. ⬭ torn
    ⬭ turn
    ⬭ tune

© Pearson Education 1

School + Home   **Home Activity** Your child read words spelled with *er*, *ir*, and *ur* that have the same vowel sound as *bird*. Help your child make up rhymes using words with this vowel sound spelled *er*, *ir*, *ur*. For example, *You can't wear that shirt. It is covered in dirt!*

Name _____

Look at each picture.
Circle the sentence that best tells about the picture.

I. Mom shouted at the dog.
   The dog has the dinner.

2. The caterpillar ate the leaf.
   The leaf is green.

3. The puppy met a skunk!
   The skunk is black and white.

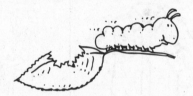

4. The bus will go to school.
   Steve had to hurry to the bus.

Look at the picture. **Answer** the question.
How does the girl feel?

_____

5. _____

_____

_____

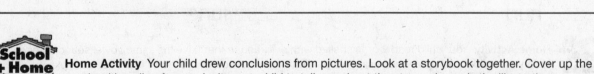

Home Activity Your child drew conclusions from pictures. Look at a storybook together. Cover up the words with a slip of paper. Invite your child to tell you about the story using only the illustrations.

44 **Comprehension** Draw Conclusions   **Practice Book Unit 3**

Name _____

Pick a word from the box that means the same as each pair of words. **Write** it on the line.

<u>She is</u> tall.
<u>She's</u> tall.

he's	it's	I've	that's	they're
they've	we're	we've	you're	you've

1. I + have

   _____
   - - - - - - -
   _____

2. we + are

   _____
   - - - - - - -
   _____

3. it + is

   _____
   - - - - - - -
   _____

4. that + is

   _____
   - - - - - - -
   _____

5. you + have

   _____
   - - - - - - -
   _____

6. they + have

   _____
   - - - - - - -
   _____

7. we + have

   _____
   - - - - - - -
   _____

8. he + is

   _____
   - - - - - - -
   _____

9. they + are

   _____
   - - - - - - -
   _____

10. you + are

   _____
   - - - - - - -
   _____

© Pearson Education 1

School + Home **Home Activity** Your child practiced making contractions with *'s*, *'ve*, and *'re*. Read each contraction on this page aloud. Challenge your child to use each one in a sentence. Then work together to write each sentence.

Name _____

Pick a word from the box to finish each sentence.
Write the words in the puzzles.

push   visit   wait

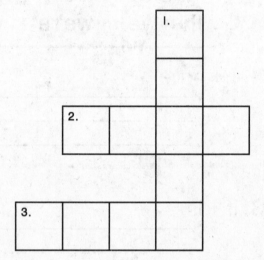

1. We'll _____ our friends soon.

2. They will _____ us on the swings.

3. I can not _____ !

---

done   know

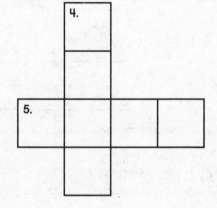

4. I _____ we will do well!

5. We will try to win. We will be happy when we are _____ .

Home Activity Your child learned to read the words *done, know, push, visit,* and *wait.* Write the words on a sheet of paper. Give your child a clue for each word. Then have him or her guess the word and point to it.

46 High-Frequency Words

Practice Book Unit 3

© Pearson Education 1

Name _____

Pick a word from the box to finish each sentence.
Write it on the line.

| done   know   push   visit   wait |

_____
- -
1. I _____ a caterpillar comes from an egg and can crawl.

_____
- -
2. I _____ a chrysalis each day.

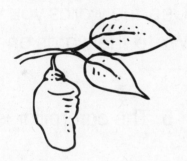

_____
- -
3. It is hard to _____ for the pupa to grow.

_____
- -
4. The chrysalis will shiver, and the pupa will _____ its way out.

_____
- -
5. It is beautiful when it is _____ .

© Pearson Education 1

School + Home **Home Activity** Your child learned to read the words *caterpillar, chrysalis, crawl, done, know, pupa, push, shiver, visit,* and *wait.* Ask your child to use each word in a spoken sentence.

Name _____

Add -ing to each word.
Write the new word on the line.

_____   _____
------------------------------   ------------------------------
1. sit _____   **2.** nap _____

Add -ed to each word.
Write the new word on the line.

_____   _____
------------------------------   ------------------------------
3. dot _____   **4.** hop _____

Use the words you wrote to finish the sentences.
Write the words on the lines.

_____
----
5. The caterpillar is _____ .

_____
----
6. The butterfly has _____ wings.

_____
----
7. The butterfly _____ to a rock.

_____
----
8. It is _____ on a plant.

School + Home   **Home Activity** Your child reviewed words that end with *-ed* and *-ing*. Read a storybook with your child and look for words that end in *-ed*. Have your child use each word you find in a new sentence. Repeat with words that end in *-ing*.

© Pearson Education 1

Name _____

Circle a word to finish each sentence.
Write it on the line.

g**ar**den

yard   yak

_____

- -

1. What is that in the _____ ?

base   bark

_____

- -

2. Look on the tree _____ !

harm   ham

_____

- -

3. It will not _____ you.

large   lung

_____

- -

4. It is eating the _____ leaf.

pork   park

_____

- -

5. One day it will fly to a _____ .

© Pearson Education 1

Home Activity Your child reviewed words with *ar* that have the sound heard in *garden*. Work with your child to make a list of words that rhyme with *bark* and *yard*.

Name _____

Look at the computer parts and labels.
Read each sentence.
Write the letter of the
part the sentence
tells about.

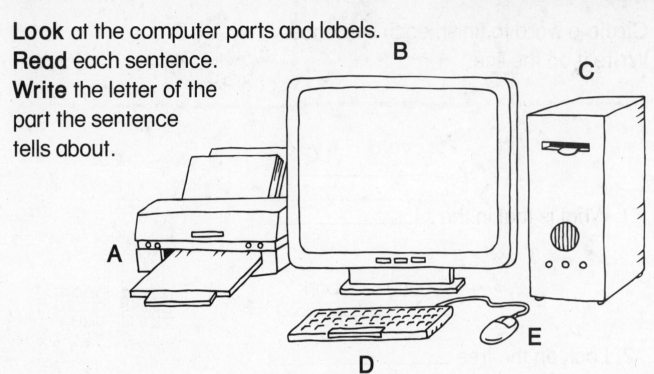

_____
_____ Use the monitor to view your file.
_____

_____ Use the mouse to click files and Web links.
_____

_____ Use the keyboard to type letters and numbers.
_____

_____ Use the disk drive to insert a disk.
_____

_____ Use the printer to print your file.

School + Home **Home Activity** Your child identified the parts and uses of a computer. If possible, use a computer with your child to give him or her more practice with these skills.

Family Times

You are your child's first and best teacher!

This week we're

Reading Where Are My
Animal Friends?

Where do animals go
when the days turn cold?

Talking About How nature changes
during the year

Learning About Comparative Endings
dge/j/
Sequence of Events

---

*Here are ways to help your child practice
skills while having fun!*

Day 1

Write these words on cards: *sad, sadder,
saddest, hot, hotter, hottest, cold, colder,
coldest, slow, slower, slowest.* Together, sort
the words according to words that double the
consonant when *-er* or *-est* are added.

Day 2

Write each word on a card: *fudge, hedge, judge,
ledge, pledge, wedge.* Have your child read
the words. Then work together to make up a
sentence using each word.

Day 3

Write the following words in a list: *before,
does, good-bye, oh, right, won't.* Together, write
a short story using the words.

Day 4

Write each spelling word on a card: *bigger,
biggest, faster, fastest, slower, slowest, shorter,
shortest, sadder, saddest, good-bye, before.* Sort
the words into piles by *more* and *most*.

Day 5

This week your child is learning to identify
sequence of events. After reading, have your
child tell you what happened in the story.

Spin It

Materials paper, paper clip, pencil, marker, 1 button per player

Game Directions

1. Make a simple spinner as shown. Players place buttons on Start.

2. Take turns spinning. Move forward that number of spaces on the game board.

3. Read the word in the space. Name the word created by adding *-er* to that word. Name the word created by adding *-est* to that word. If you can tell correctly whether or not the final consonant must be doubled to add *-er* or *-est*, move ahead one space. Play passes to the next player. The game continues until all players reach End.

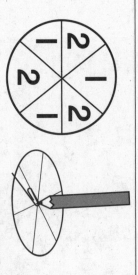

Answers:

hard, harder, hardest (no); sad, sadder, saddest (yes); thin, thinner, thinnest (yes); flat, flatter, flattest (yes); short, shorter, shortest (no); red, redder, reddest (yes); green, greener, greenest (no); tall, taller, tallest (no); small, smaller, smallest (no); big, bigger, biggest (yes); wet, wetter, wettest (yes); old, older, oldest (no); fast, faster, fastest (no); slow, slower, slowest (no)

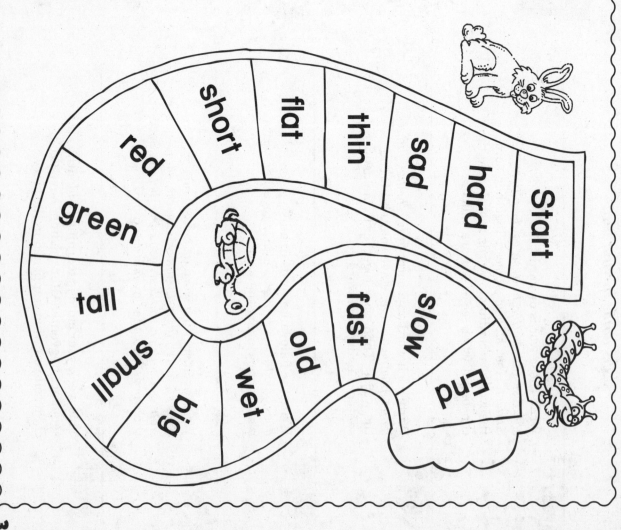

Name _____

Circle the word for each picture.

small   small**er**   small**est**

I.

faster   fastest

2.

bigger   biggest

3.

taller   tallest

4.

sweeter   sweetest

5.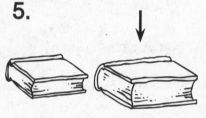

thicker   thickest

6.

thinner   thinnest

Write -er or **-est** to finish the word in each sentence.

7. The little bird has the few _____ eggs.

8. The little bird has a long _____ tail than
   the big bird.

School + Home   **Home Activity** Your child identified the comparative endings *-er* and *-est* as in *smaller* and *smallest*. Discuss the sizes, shapes, and colors of animals. Have your child compare the animals using *-er* when comparing two and *-est* when comparing more than two.

© Pearson Education 1

Name _____

Read the story. **Look** at the pictures.

Write 1, 2, 3 to show the right order.

It was spring.

The mother goose flew in.

She made a nest.

There were five eggs.

The mother goose swam with her little ones.

1. ☐

2. ☐

3. ☐

Draw a picture to show what happened before.

4.

Draw a picture to show what happens next.

5.

 School + Home **Home Activity** Your child learned about the order in which events happen in a story. As you read stories together, have your child tell you what is happening in the story, what came before, and what could happen next.

54 **Comprehension** Sequence of Events

Name _____

Pick a word from the box to finish each sentence.
Write it on the line.

| fudge | hedge | judge | ledge | smudge |

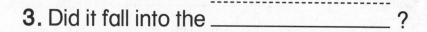

badge

_____
- - - - - - - - - - - - - - - - -
1. Mom made _____ for us to eat.

_____
- - - - - - - - - - - - - - - -
2. She set it on the _____ .

_____
- - - - - - - - - - - - - - - -
3. Did it fall into the _____ ?

_____
- - - - - - - - - - - - - - - -
4. Look, there's a _____ on Bear's face.

_____
- - - - - - - - - - - - - - -
5. The _____
thinks Bear ate it too.

Home Activity Your child learned to read words that end with *dge* that have the sound heard in *judge*. Have your child make a list of words that rhyme with *judge* (*budge, fudge, nudge, grudge, smudge, trudge*).

Practice Book Unit 3

Name _____

Pick a word from the box that is the opposite of each word below.
Write it on the line.

| before good-bye right won't |

1. after

_____

2. will

_____

3. hello

_____

4. wrong

_____

$$\begin{array}{r} 2 \\ +2 \\ \hline =4 \end{array}$$

Pick a word from the box to finish each sentence.
Write it on the line. **Remember** to use capital letters.

| oh does |

5. _____ a bear start its long sleep in the spring?

6. _____ , no. It sleeps when the days start to get cold.

© Pearson Education 1

Home Activity Your child learned to read the words *before, does, good-bye, oh, right,* and *won't*. Write the opposite of these words on cards and mix them up. Have your child match the words that are opposites and then read the pairs. Then have him or her write two sentences using *does* and *oh*.

Name _____

Read the words in the box.
Match a word from the box to each clue in the puzzle. **Write** it.

| before   does   good-bye   goose   oh   right   won't |

1. Winter is the _____ season for mittens.

2. When _____ it start to get warm?

3. In spring we say _____ to cold days.

4. _____ ! How I love to see the trees turn green.

5. Then, _____ long, the days grow warmer!

6. It _____ be long before I see a raccoon peeking out at dusk.

7. I may even see a _____ with white feathers.

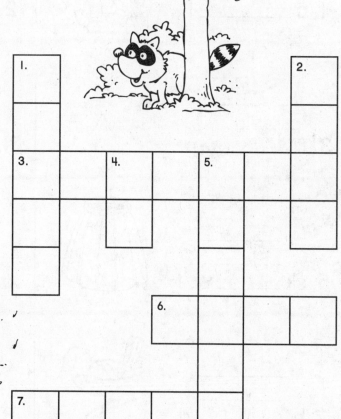

Home Activity Your child learned to read the words *before, does, good-bye, goose, oh, raccoon, right, spring, warm,* and *won't*. Write each word on a small piece of paper. Have your child choose a word and use it in a sentence about a season. Repeat this process with the other words.

Name _____

Pick the letters from the box to finish each word.
Write the letters on the line.

$$\boxed{\text{er} \quad \text{ir} \quad \text{ur}}$$

1. c _____ l

2. f _____ st

3. f _____ n

4. d _____ t

5. sk _____ t

6. h _____

7. b _____ d

8. b _____ n

9. cl _____ k

10. h _____ t

Home Activity Your child reviewed words with *er, ir,* and *ur* that have the sound heard in *term, shirt,* and *turtle.* Make a list of *er, ir,* and *ur* words that have this vowel sound, such as *fern, her, dirt, bird, curl,* and *burn.* Ask your child to sort the words by their spelling.

© Pearson Education 1

Name _____

Write the contraction for each pair of words.

1. we + have = _____

2. he + is = _____

3. I + have = _____

4. they + have = _____

5. that + is = _____

6. it + is = _____

7. you + are = _____

8. you + have = _____

Here is my balloon.
Here's my balloon.

Find the contraction.
Mark the ⬭ to show your answer.

9. ⬭ she's
   ⬭ she
   ⬭ sons

10. ⬭ were
    ⬭ we're
    ⬭ went

Home Activity Your child reviewed contractions—words made up of two words and an apostrophe. Write the words *he, she, it, is, they, you, have,* and *are* on pieces of paper. Ask your child to see how many different contractions he or she can form.

Name _____

Use the bar graph to answer the questions.

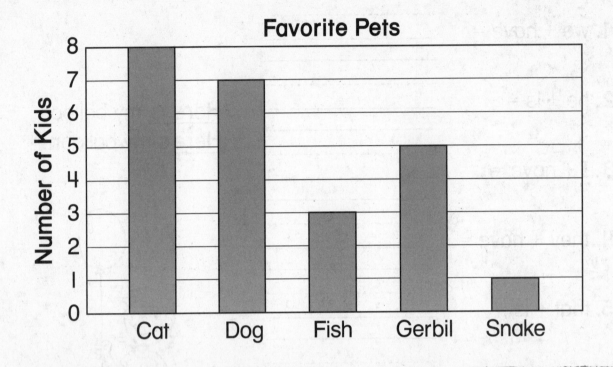

Favorite Pets

1. What does the graph show?

_____

- -

_____

2. How many kids like fish? _____

3. How many kids like gerbils? _____

4. Which kind of pet is most liked? _____

5. Which kind of pet is least liked? _____

Home Activity Your child learned to read a bar graph. Together, make a bar graph that displays information about your family, such as the favorite foods of each member.

Name

Family Times

You are your child's first and best teacher!

This week we're

Reading Mama's Birthday Present

Mama's Birthday Present

by Carmen Tafolla
Illustrated by Gabriel Pacheco

14

What is Mama's birthday present?

15

Talking About How a surprise can
be a treasure

Learning About Long *a*: *ai*, *ay*
Possessives
Draw Conclusions

© Pearson Education 1

*Here are ways to help your child practice
skills while having fun!*

Day 1

Help your child write sentences, using as
many *ai* and *ay* words as possible. Some words
to use are: *main, wait, paid, aim, day, stay.*

Day 2

Write each word on a card: *Kris's, Jake's,
Sam's, Kate's, the Smith Family's, the first
graders', the lions', the dogs'.* Take turns
picking a card and thinking of something for
that person, persons, or animals to possess.

Day 3

Write the following words in a list: *about,
enjoy, give, surprise, worry, would.* Together
write a story about a surprise party.

Day 4

Write each spelling word on a card: *train, way,
tail, play, day, may, rain, gray, mail, afraid.*
Have your child sort the words into piles by *ai*
and *ay.* Then have your child read the words
and spell them aloud.

Day 5

This week your child is learning to draw
conclusions using the text as well as what he
or she already knows. As you read, stop often
and discuss what ideas the author may be
saying indirectly.

One Rainy Day

Materials paper, pencil, paper clip, index cards, 1 button per player

Game Directions

1. Prepare a set of word cards: *aim, gain, rail, main, nail, paid, pain, paid, sail, wait, day, gray, hay, may, maybe, play, say, stay, today, way.* Sort the words into *ai* and *ay* piles. Prepare a spinner as shown below.

2. Place markers at Start. Players take turns spinning the spinner, moving their button the number of spaces indicated, and then picking a card from the indicated pile. If the player can read the word card correctly, then he or she stays on that space. If not, the player goes back two spaces.

3. If players land in a mud puddle, they must go back one space. If they land on hot chocolate, the other player must go back one space.

4. Play continues until a player reaches End.

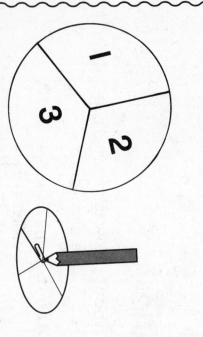

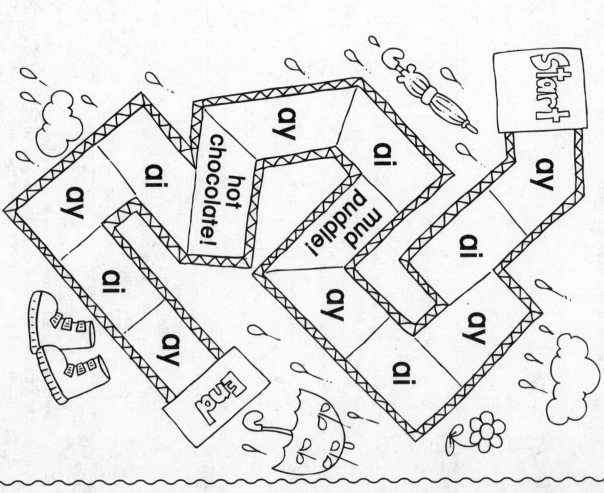

Name _____

t<u>ai</u>l   pl<u>ay</u>

Circle the word for each picture.

1. 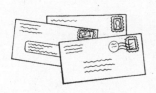	2. 	3. 	4. 
mail mall	tray tree	pal pail	pan pain

5. 	6. 	7. 	8. 
sell sail	he hay	train trap	page pay

Find the word that has the same **long a** sound as .
Mark the ⬭ to show your answer.

9. ⬭ clip
   ⬭ clap
   ⬭ clay

10. ⬭ man
    ⬭ main
    ⬭ mine

 Home Activity Your child read words in which the long *a* sound is spelled *ai* and *ay,* as in *rain* and *hay.* Ask your child to name a rhyming word for each long *a* word on this page.

Practice Book Unit 4 **Phonics** Long *a: ai, ay* **63**

Name _____

Look at the picture.
Circle the sentence that tells about the picture.

1.

Dad is happy about his new shed from Jen.
Jen is happy about her tree house from Dad.

2.

They planted a garden.

Flowers grow in gardens.

3.

We are singing in the play.
The class sets up for a play.

4.

Tom is good at running.
Tom is a good friend.

Write a sentence about the picture.

5.

_____

- -

_____

- -

© Pearson Education 1

School + Home

Home Activity Your child drew conclusions from pictures. Look at a story with your child. Cover up the words with paper. Invite your child to tell you about the story using only the illustrations.

Name _____

Write each word correctly.
Use 's or ' at the end of each word.

Meg<u>'s</u> hat

1. Janes drum = _____ drum

2. dogs bones = _____ bones

3. Moms cup = _____ cup

4. babys crib = _____ crib

5. pets beds = _____ beds

Pick a word from the box to match each picture.
Write it on the line.

 girls'   Matt's

6. _____ lunch

7. _____ games

Home Activity Your child wrote words that show ownership. Point out objects in your home that are owned by one or more persons in the family. Ask your child to use a possessive to tell you who owns each object (*Mike's pen*).

Practice Book Unit 4

Phonics Possessives **65**

© Pearson Education 1

Name _____

Pick a word from the box to match each clue set.
Look at the scrambled letters for a hint.
Write the word on the line.

> about   enjoy   gives   surprise
> surprised   worry   would

1. I _____ helping. **nyjeo**

2. We eat at _____ 12:00. **buato**

3. _____ you please help me? **odluw**

4. Do not _____ . I will help. **woryr**

5. When we jump up, she will be _____ . **sipresrud**

6. Dad _____ us gifts. **ivseg**

7. The gifts are always a big _____ . **rrpsiues**

Home Activity Your child learned to read the words *about, enjoy, gives, surprise, surprised, worry,* and *would.* Ask your child to use these words to create a puppet show with paper bag puppets. Record the script on paper and have your child practice reading it aloud.

Name _____

Pick a word from the box to finish each sentence.
Write it on the line.

> about enjoy gives
> surprise surprised
> worry would

1. My mom will _____ about the party.

2. She _____ like to have buñuelos, but my dad likes a plain tortilla.

3. It will be a _____ . We will have confetti.

4. My dad likes to be _____ .

5. He will _____ the guitar I got him for a present.

6. He _____ us so much. Now we can give back.

7. He will talk _____ the piñata and the wonderful party all week.

Home Activity Your child learned to read the words *about, buñuelos, confetti, enjoy, gives, guitar, piñata, present, tortilla, surprise, surprised, wonderful, worry,* and *would.* Write the words. Have your child read one word at a time and use each word in a spoken sentence.

Name _____

Circle the word for each picture.

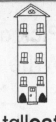

tall   tall**er**   tall**est**

1.

fatter   fattest

2.

thinner   thinnest

3.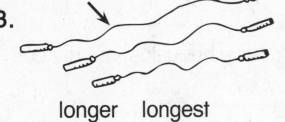

longer   longest

4.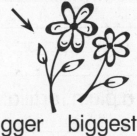

bigger   biggest

5.

older   oldest

6.

hotter   hottest

Find the word that could be used to compare **two** things.
Mark the ⬭ to show your answer.

7. ⬭ few
   ⬭ fewer
   ⬭ fewest

8. ⬭ green
   ⬭ greener
   ⬭ greenest

© Pearson Education 1

 Home Activity Your child reviewed words with the comparative endings *-er* and *-est*. With your child, look at family photos or photos in catalogs or magazines. Ask your child to compare people or objects using words with *-er* or *-est* endings.

Name _____

Pick a word from the box to finish each sentence.
Write it on the line.

le**dge**

| fudge | hedge | nudge | smudge | wedge |

_____
- -
1. Dad set out a _____ of cheese.

_____
- -
2. He put out a plate of _____ .

_____
- -
3. There is a _____ on the banner.

_____
- -
4. We put the banner on the _____ .

_____
- -
5. With a _____ I yelled, "Surprise!"

School + Home **Home Activity** Your child reviewed words that end with *dge* that have the sound heard in *fudge*. Have your child write and sort the words from the box into two lists of rhyming words. Help your child add one new word to each list.

© Pearson Education 1

Name _____

Write the days of the week in order.

> **Saturday   Thursday   Monday   Wednesday**
> **Sunday   Friday   Tuesday**

1. _____   2. _____

3. _____   4. _____

5. _____   6. _____

7. _____

Pick a month from the box to finish each sentence.
Write it on the line.

> **July   November   February**

8. We make a [card] in _____ .

9. It may get hot in _____ .

10. Thanksgiving Day is in _____ .

© Pearson Education 1

 Home Activity Your child learned about the days of the week and months of the year. Work with your child to locate upcoming events on a calendar.

Name

Family Times

You are your child's first and best teacher!

This week we're

Reading The Dot

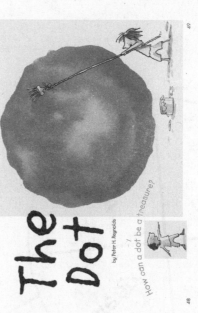

The Dot

by Peter H. Reynolds

How can a dot be a treasure?

48

49

Talking About Treasures we can create

Learning About Long *e*: *ea*
Inflected Endings
Theme

Here are ways to help your child practice skills while having fun!

Day 1

Take turns writing one of these *ea* words and then illustrating it: *leaf, seal, bean, stream, beads, seat.*

Day 2

Write these words one at a time: *dry, copy, spy, cry, try, worry.* Then have your child add -ed to the word, making sure to change the *y* to *i* before writing the new word.

Day 3

Write the following words: *colors, draw, drew, great, over, show, sign.* Have your child dictate a sentence for each word. Then ask your child to read the sentences back to you.

Day 4

Write each spelling word in large letters: *eat, sea, each, team, please, dream, treat, beach, clean, lean.* Have your child read each word aloud. With a crayon, trace over the *ea* together as your child spells the words.

Day 5

This week your child is learning about the theme, or the big idea, in a story. As you read together, discuss the big idea of the story.

Read for Speed

Materials crayons

Game Directions

1. Players take turns reading a word in a bicycle wheel.

2. Color *long e: ea* words yellow. Color *long e: ee* words red.

3. Continue until all spaces are colored.

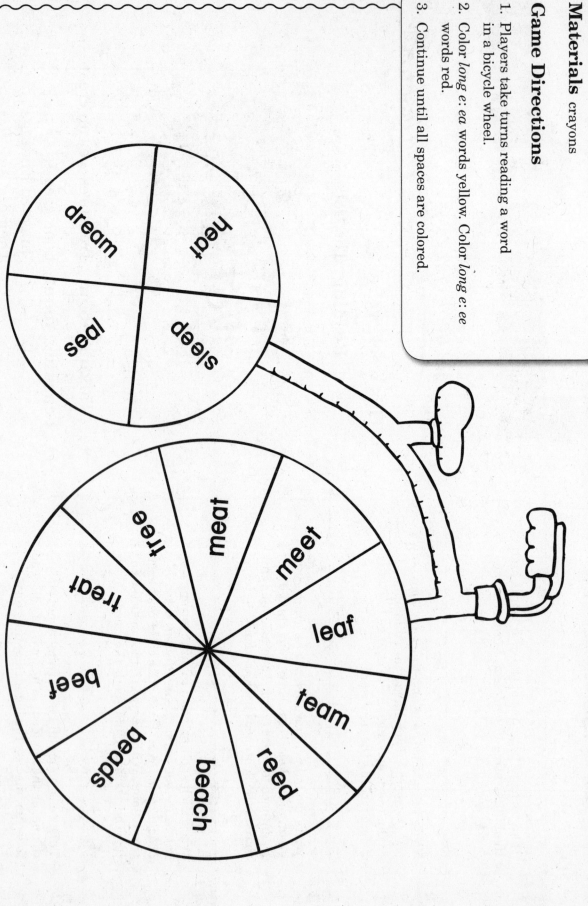

Name _____

Circle the word for each picture.

 b**ea**n

1.

peas   pets

2.

bride   bead

3.

sail   seal

4.

birch   beach

5.

leaf   loaf

6.

jeans   jars

7.

bake   beak

8.

clean   clang

Find the word that has the same **long e** sound as .
Mark the ⬭ to show your answer.

9. ⬭ peak
   ⬭ pack
   ⬭ peck

10. ⬭ wove
    ⬭ wave
    ⬭ weave

© Pearson Education 1

 School +Home   **Home Activity** Your child read words in which the long *e* sound is spelled *ea*. Ask your child to think of rhyming words for the words on this page. Write each word and review the vowel spelling together.

Name _____

Read the story.

Write a sentence that tells the big idea.

Draw a picture of the big idea.

Rainy Day

It was not a sunny day. Ben went out to play in the rain. Ben stepped in the water on the ground. He jumped and water flew. Ben grinned. Splish! Splash!

2.

1. _____

Read the big idea.

Draw a picture in the box to show the big idea.

Big Idea: It is fun to make art.

Write a title for your picture.

3.

4. _____

Home Activity Your child learned about the theme, or the big idea, in a story. Read a story from a collection of fables. Discuss with your child the big idea, or moral, of each story.

© Pearson Education 1

Name _____

Add **-ed** to each word.
Write the new words on the line.

 fr**ied**

Add -ed

1. dry
_____
- - - - - - - - - - - - - -
_____

2. cry
_____
- - - - - - - - - - - - - -
_____

3. spy
_____
- - - - - - - - - - - - - -
_____

4. worry
_____
- - - - - - - - - - - - - -
_____

5. try
_____
- - - - - - - - - - - - - -
_____

6. copy
_____
- - - - - - - - - - - - - -
_____

Add **-er** and **-est** to each word.
Write the new words on the line.

	Add -er	**Add -est**
7. silly		
8. funny		
9. happy		
10. easy		

School + Home

Home Activity Your child practiced adding endings to words where the spelling changed from *y* to *i* before adding *-ed, -er,* or *-est.* Use the words above to make up a story with your child.

Name _____

Pick a word from the box to finish each sentence.
Write it on the line.

> colors   draw   drew   great   over   show   sign

_____
\- - - - - - - - - - - - - - - - - - -
1. I like to _____ .

_____
\- - - - - - - - - - - - - - -
2. I want to _____ my art to my friend.

_____
\- - - - - - - - - - - - - - -
3. Yesterday I _____ a sun and trees for her.

_____
\- - - - - - - - - - - - - - -
4. I used many _____ .

_____
\- - - - - - - - - - - - - - -
5. She will think it is _____ .

_____
\- - - - - - - - - - - - - - -
6. I will _____ the back.

_____
\- - - - - - - - - - - - - - -
7. When she turns it _____ , she will see my name.

![Molly drawing]

© Pearson Education 1

School + Home **Home Activity** Your child learned to read the words *colors, draw, drew, great, over, show,* and *sign*. Have your child make up a sentence using each word as you write the sentences on paper. Then ask him or her to read the sentences back to you.

Name _____

Pick a word from the box to finish each sentence.
Write it on the line.

> colors   draw   drew   great
> over   show   sign

---

1. We are experimenting with new _____ .

2. His gold circles are _____ .

3. I made a long squiggle _____ a short yellow splash.

4. I stared at the shapes the artist _____ .

5. Can you _____ shapes with straight lines?

6. I will _____ you how to do it.

7. When we are done, we will _____ each painting.

Home Activity Your child learned to read the words *artist, colors, draw, drew, experimenting, gold, great, over, sign, show, splash(ed), stared, squiggle,* and *straight.* Point to each of these words. Ask your child to read the word and use it in a spoken sentence.

© Pearson Education 1

Name _____

Write the word for each picture.

 n<u>ai</u>l   h<u>ay</u>

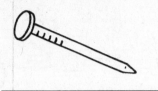

_____   _____

1. Put the _____ in the _____ .

_____   _____

2. Does a _____ have a _____ ?

Circle the word in each sentence that has the **long a** sound.

3. Steve likes to paint.

4. Steve keeps his colors in a tray.

5. He uses the color gray.

6. It is a good color for rain.

School + Home

Home Activity Your child reviewed words with the long *a* sound spelled *ai* and *ay*. Make a rhyme with your child using words with *ay* and *ai*. Examples: *A jay likes to play in the hay* or *Can a chain pull a train?*

Name _____

Look at each picture.
Add 's to a word to show who owns something.
Write the new word on the line.

1.

_____

_____ mug

2.

_____

_____ bib

3.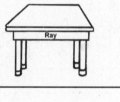

_____

_____ desk

4.

_____

_____ tree

5.

_____

_____ ball

6.

_____

_____ dish

Find the words that tell who owns something.
Mark the ⬭ to show your answer.

7. ⬭ girls paints
   ⬭ girls's paints
   ⬭ girls' paints

8. ⬭ boys' shoes
   ⬭ boys's shoes
   ⬭ boys shoes

 Home Activity Your child used 's (singular) and s' (plural) to tell who owns something. Draw pictures together of objects that belong to people in your family. Help your child label each picture, such as *Carmen's shirt* or *the kids' beds*.

© Pearson Education 1

Use the chart to answer the questions.

Tickets	
Monday	ⵜⵜⵜ
Tuesday	IIII
Wednesday	III
Thursday	II
Friday	ⵜⵜⵜ I

ⵜⵜⵜ = 5

1. On which day did the children sell 5 tickets to the Art Show?

_____

- -

_____

2. Did the children sell more tickets on Monday or Friday?

_____

- -

_____

3. On which day were the fewest tickets sold?

_____

- -

_____

4. How many tickets were sold on Wednesday and Thursday?

_____

- -

_____

© Pearson Education 1

School + Home

Home Activity Your child used a chart to find information and answer questions. Together, create a chart showing chores that family members do at home.

Family Times

You are your child's first and best teacher!

This week we're

Reading Mister Bones:
Dinosaur Hunter

Talking About Treasures we can find
in the earth

Learning About Long *o*: *oa, ow*
Three-letter Blends
Author's Purpose

---

*Here are ways to help your child practice
skills while having fun!*

 Day 1

Write these long *o* words: *load, float, toast, show*. One player reads a word, and the other thinks of one or more rhyming words.

 Day 2

Write the following three letter blends in red on index cards: *scr, spl, squ, str*. Write the following word parts in blue on other cards: *ap, ub, ash, int, are, eeze, ing, eam*. Together, match up the blends to the word endings to make real words.

 Day 3

Write the following words in a list: *found, mouth, once, took, wild*. Take turns picking one of the words and making up a riddle to help the other players guess the chosen word.

 Day 4

Write each spelling word on a card: *boat, road, snow, row, yellow, loaf, coat, soap, blow, pillow*. Have your child read the words. Then take turns dictating a word and writing it.

 Day 5

This week your child is learning to think about why an author might have written a story. As you read stories together, stop and discuss why the author might have decided to write them.

Row Your Boat!

Materials paper circle, paper clip, pencils, 1 button per player

Game Directions

1. Make a simple spinner as shown. On a large sheet of paper, make a game path in the shape of a stream with 12 spaces. Make boat cards like the ones shown on page 3 using the words at the bottom of page 3. Shuffle them and place them in a pile next to the game path.

2. Before spinning, a player picks a boat card and reads aloud the word on the card. If the word is read correctly, then he or she spins and moves the number of spaces shown on the spinner. Players get one turn per spin. If the word is read incorrectly, play passes to the next player, and the card goes back to the bottom of the pile.

3. The first player to reach End wins!

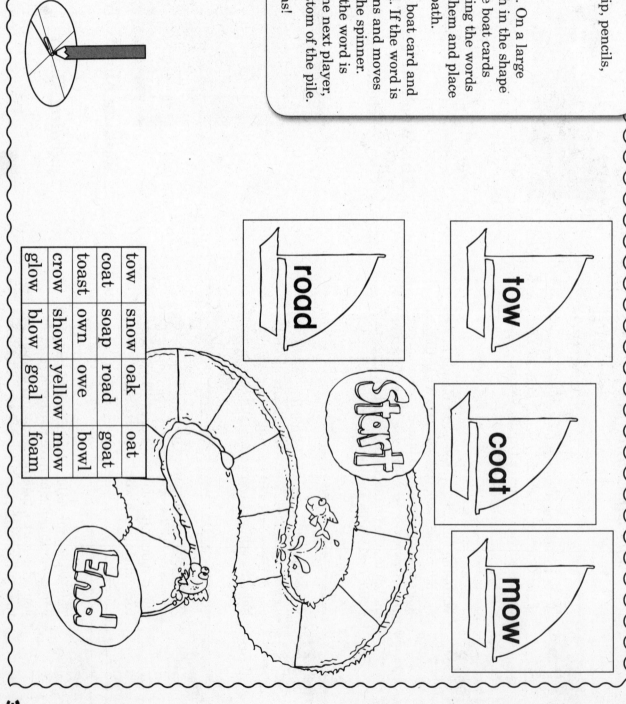

tow	snow	oak	oat
coat	soap	road	goat
toast	own	owe	bowl
crow	show	yellow	mow
glow	blow	goal	foam

Name _____

Circle the word for each picture.

 <u>toa</u>d

 bl<u>ow</u>

1. 	2. 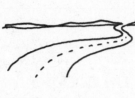	3. 	4. 
snap snow	road rod	boat beat	sap soap

5. 	6. 	7. 	8.
bee bow	coat cot	ray row	leaf loaf

Find the word that has the same **long o** sound as  .
Mark the ⬭ to show your answer.

9. ⬭ got
   ⬭ goal
   ⬭ gal

10. ⬭ low
    ⬭ lost
    ⬭ late

Home Activity Your child read words in which the long o sound is spelled *oa* and *ow*, as in *toad* and *blow*. Together, list as many words as possible with the long o sound in their names. Then ask your child to sort the words by their spellings.

© Pearson Education 1

Name _____

Look at this book.
Circle or **write** your answers.

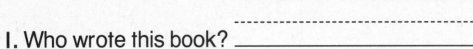

1. Who wrote this book? _____

2. What do you think this book will be about?

   things on ships   things on the beach   fish

3. What do you think is in this book?

   jokes   bears   beach facts

4. Why do you think Pam wrote this book?

   to tell facts   to make you sad   to be funny

5. Would you want to read this book? Why or why not?

_____

_____

_____

_____

© Pearson Education 1

**School + Home** **Home Activity** Your child learned about why an author may have written a story. Before reading a story together, have your child look at the cover and the pictures inside. Then ask questions like the ones on this page.

Circle the word for each picture.

1.
   stub
   scrub

2.
   splash
   slash

3.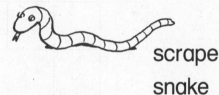
   squeeze
   sneeze

4.
   sting
   string

5.
   lint
   splint

6.
   spring
   sing

7.
   scrape
   snake

8.
   stripe
   ripe

Find the word that has the same beginning sounds as the picture.
Mark the ⬭ to show your answer.

9. ⬭ spare
   ⬭ square
   ⬭ snare

10. ⬭ stream
    ⬭ cream
    ⬭ scream

© Pearson Education 1

Home Activity Your child read words that begin with three-letter blends. Have your child draw pictures of *screen, spray, squint,* and *street.* Have him or her label each picture with the word.

Name _____

Pick a word from the box to finish each sentence.
Write it in the puzzle.

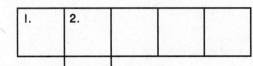

found   mouth   once   took   wild

1. You talk with your _____ .

 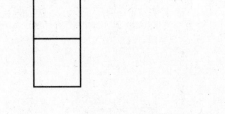

Fairy Tales

2. "_____ upon a time . . ."

3. not lost

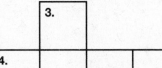

4. He _____ three bites
of his cake.

5. A raccoon is a _____ animal.

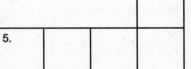

© Pearson Education 1

School + Home **Home Activity** Your child learned to read the words *found, mouth, once, took,* and *wild*. Ask your child to write and illustrate a fairy tale about a boy or girl who finds a wild animal. Encourage your child to use the new words and help him or her with spelling if necessary.

Name _____

Pick a word from the box to finish each sentence.
Write it on the line. **Remember** to use a capital letter at the beginning of a sentence.

> cowboy   found   mouth   once   took   wild

_____
----
1. _____ upon a time there was a cowboy.

_____
----
2. The _____ wore two bandannas around his neck.

_____
----
3. One day in Montana, he _____ a gigantic gold lizard!

_____
----
4. The tyrant had a huge _____ .

_____
----
5. The cowboy _____ the lizard to a museum.

_____
----
6. The museum traded the cowboy a _____ horse for the lizard.

Home Activity Your child learned to read the words *bandannas, cowboy, found, gigantic, lizard, Montana, mouth, museum, once, took, tyrant,* and *wild.* Ask your child to tell a story about a Montana cowboy. Write down the story and have him or her illustrate it.

Name _____

Circle a word to finish each sentence.
Write it on the line.

p**ea**ch

sack   sea

_____

- - - - - - - - - - - - - - - - -

1. We went down to the _____ .

beach   bash

_____

- - - - - - - - - - - - - - - - -

2. We walked on the _____ .

note   neat

_____

- - - - - - - - - - - - - - - - -

3. We put shells in _____ rows.

reach   rash

_____

- - - - - - - - - - - - - - - - -

4. I can't _____ that one!

clean   clan

_____

- - - - - - - - - - - - - - - - -

5. We _____ off the sand.

Home Activity Your child reviewed words with the long *e* sound spelled *ea* as in *peach*. Work with your child to make a list of other words with the long *e* sound spelled *ea*. Ask him or her to rhyme the new words with the words in these sentences.

© Pearson Education 1

Name _____

Add -ed to each word.　　　　　cry　　　　cr**ied**
Write the new word on the line.

_____　　　　_____
- - - - - - - - - - - - - - - - -　　　- - - - - - - - - - - - - - - - -
1. carry _____　　2. pry _____

Add -er and **-est** to each word.　　happy　happi**er**　happi**est**
Write the new words on the line.

_____　　　　_____
- - - - - - - - - - - - - - - - -　　　- - - - - - - - - - - - - - - - -
easy　　3. _____　　4. _____

_____　　　　_____
- - - - - - - - - - - - - - - - -　　　- - - - - - - - - - - - - - - - -
pretty　5. _____　　6. _____

Use some of the words you wrote to finish the sentences.
Write the words on the lines.

_____
- - - - - - - - - - - - - - - - -
7. He _____ the bone from the mud.

_____
- - - - - - - - - - - - - - - - -
8. I _____ the bone.

_____
- - - - - - - - - - - - - - - - -
9. That was _____ than this was!

_____
- - - - - - - - - - - - - - - - -
10. My bone is the _____ one.

Home Activity Your child reviewed words with endings -ed, -er, and -est. Have your child add -ed to *dry*, *spy*, *hurry*, and *copy*. Then have him or her add -er and -est to *funny*, *messy*, *bumpy*, *lucky*, and *sunny*. Check to make sure your child made the correct spelling changes.

Name _____

Read the story.

Mike asked his friends what they liked to do on the weekends. Three of his friends liked to dance. Five of his friends liked to play soccer. Two of his friends liked to paint. One of his friends liked to skate. Four of his friends liked to read.

Fill in the bar graph to show what Mike's friends like.

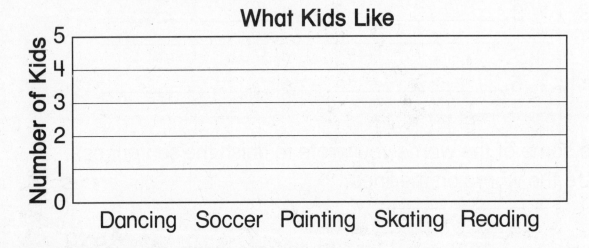

Answer the questions.

_____

1. How many friends like dancing? _____

_____

2. What is best liked? _____

_____

3. What is the least liked? _____

_____

4. How many friends like to read? _____

© Pearson Education 1

Family Times

Name

You are your child's first and best teacher!

This week we're

Reading The Lady in the Moon

The Lady in the Moon

by Lily Wong Fillmore
illustrated by Lin Wong

Who is the Lady in the Moon?

Talking About How we can share
special days

Learning About Long *i: ie, igh*
kn/n/ and *wr/r/*
Realism and Fantasy

*Here are ways to help your child practice
skills while having fun!*

Day 1

Write each word on a card: *tie, pie, high, sigh,
might, night, tight.* Challenge your child to
write a sentence for each word and then read
each sentence.

Day 2

Write these words: *knight, know, knew, knot,
knob, write, wrong, wrap, wrist, wreck.* Read
the words together. Take turns circling the
silent letter or letters in each word.

Day 3

Write the following words in a list: *above,
eight, laugh, moon, touch.* Together, read the
words aloud and then compose a story that
uses all of the words.

Day 4

Write each spelling word on a card: *lie, tie,
high, might, right, night, bright, light, pie,
tight.* Together, read the words and sort them
into groups by *ie* and *igh.*

Day 5

This week your child is learning to tell the
difference between what could and could not
happen in a story. As you read with your child
this week, stop and discuss whether the events
in the story could really happen.

How High For Pie?

Materials index cards, scissors, crayon, coin

Game Directions

1. Cut out small pie shapes and have each player write his or her name on one.

2. Each player flips the coin. If it lands heads up, the player moves his or her game piece two half-pies. If it lands tails up, the player moves it one half-pie.

3. Each player reads aloud the word on the pie. Play passes to the next person. Play continues until all the pieces reach End.

Start

high → sigh → light → might → night → right → sight → tight → tie → pie **End**

Kyle

Mike

Name _____

Circle the word for each picture.

 p<u>ie</u>   l<u>igh</u>t

1.	2.	3.	4.

night note	sit lie	tie tea	fit fight

5.	6.	7.	8.

pit pie	hay high	sit sight	tight toad

Find the word that has the **long i** sound as in
Mark the ⬭ to show your answer.   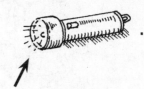 .

9. ⬭ lit
   ⬭ lie
   ⬭ list

10. ⬭ mitt
    ⬭ might
    ⬭ mill

School + Home **Home Activity** Your child practiced reading words in which the long *i* sound is spelled *igh* and *ie* as in *light* and *pie*. Encourage your child to create a poem, nonsense rhyme, or song using *igh* and *ie* words.

© Pearson Education 1

Name _____

Look at each pair of pictures.
Circle the picture that shows something that could really happen.

1.

2.

3.

4.

© Pearson Education 1

Draw a picture of something that could really happen.

5.

 Home Activity Your child made choices about events that could really happen and events that could not happen. Play a game with your child. Offer two situations: one possible and one not possible. Have your child identify which situation could really happen and which could not.

Name _____

Circle the word for each picture.

knight   **wr**ench

1. 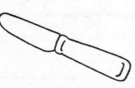	2. 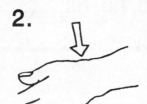	3. 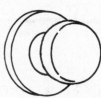	4.
knife night	rest wrist	nine knit	knob not

5. 	6. 	7. 	8. 
note knot	wreck rack	white write	ring wrong

Find the word that has the same beginning sound as the picture.
Mark the ⟨⟩ to show your answer.

9. ◯ wren
   ◯ when
   ◯ went

10. ◯ sneak
    ◯ kite
    ◯ knock

 School +Home **Home Activity** Your child read words that begin with *kn* as in *knight* and *wr* as in *wrench*. Have your child copy all the words from the page that begin with *kn* and *wr* and ask him or her to circle the silent letter in each word.

Name _____

Pick a word from the box to match each clue.
Write it on the line.

> above   eight   laugh   moon   touch

1. "Ha, ha, ha!" _____

2. five, six, seven, _____

3. 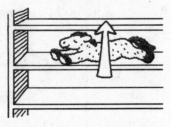 not below _____

4.  feel _____

5.  stars, planets, _____

 Home Activity Your child learned to read the words *above*, *eight*, *laugh*, *moon*, and *touch*. Act out clues for each word and have your child guess which word you picked.

© Pearson Education 1

Name _____

Pick a word from the box to finish each sentence.
Write it on the line.

> above   eight   laugh   moon
> poems   touch   treasures

_____
- -
1. Now is the _____ festival.

_____
- -
2. We give each other little moon _____ .

_____
- -
3. We toss _____ lotus leaves into the water.

_____
- -
4. We eat pears and read _____ .

_____
- -
5. _____ our window, we hang a drawing of the moon.

_____
- -
6. We play games like moon tag and _____ all day.

7. The moon is so big that we pretend we can
_____
- -
_____ it.

Home Activity Your child learned to read the words *above, eight, festival, laugh, lotus leaves, moon, pears, poems, touch* and *treasures*. Ask your child to create a play with you about a festival that uses pears, poems, lotus leaves, and treasures.

Name _____

Circle the word for each picture.
Write it on the line.

 b**oa**t  wind**ow**

1.

cat
coat
cot

_____

2.

crop
crate
crow

_____

3.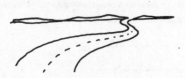

road
rod
red

_____

4.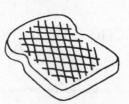

toast
tote
toss

_____

5.

mob
mow
me

_____

School + Home
Home Activity Your child reviewed words with the long *o* sound spelled *oa* as in *boat* and *ow* as in *window*.
Read each long *o* word on this page aloud. Ask your child to name a word that rhymes with each word.

Name _____

Pick letters from the box to finish each word.
Write the letters on the line.

scr squ str spl

1. _____ are

2. _____ ub

3. _____ eam

4. _____ ash

5. _____ ash

6. _____ ing

7. _____ een

8. _____ ipe

9. _____ int

10. _____ atch

Home Activity Your child reviewed words that begin with three-letter blends. Have your child read each word and use it in a sentence.

Name _____

Read the guide words.
Write the word from the box that
you would find on that page.

> tag bed send hot cat

1. hat   hunt

_____

- - - - - - - - - - - - - - - -

2. bag   box

_____

- - - - - - - - - - - - - - - -

3. book   cut

_____

- - - - - - - - - - - - - - - -

4. sack   tend

_____

- - - - - - - - - - - - - - - -

> dog feed gone lip mint

5. let   lock

_____

- - - - - - - - - - - - - - - -

6. day   duck

_____

- - - - - - - - - - - - - - - -

7. gas   gust

_____

- - - - - - - - - - - - - - - -

8. man   mole

_____

- - - - - - - - - - - - - - - -

Home Activity Your child learned about using alphabetical order and guide words in a dictionary. Look through a children's dictionary with your child. Make a game of finding new words by using the guide words at the top of each page.

Family Times

You are your child's first and best teacher!

This week we're

Reading Peter's Chair

What is special about Peter's chair?

PETER'S CHAIR
by Ezra Jack Keats

Talking About Treasures we can share at home

Learning About Compound Words
Vowels *ew, ue, ui*
Character, Setting, and Plot

Here are ways to help your child practice skills while having fun!

Day 1

Write the following words on cards: *seaweed, seesaw, beanbag, beehive, anthill, baseball.* Cut each word in half to make two small words. Shuffle the cards and together match them to find the compound words.

Day 2

Have your child write sentences for the following words: *few, new, blue, true, suit, fruit.* Ask your child to read the sentences. Together, pick your favorite sentence and draw an illustration for it.

Day 3

Write the following words on cards: *picture, remember, room, stood, thought.* Hide the cards around the house. When your child finds a word card, he or she can take it to you and read it.

Day 4

Write each spelling word on a card: *backpack, outside, baseball, herself, flashlight, bluebird, lunchbox, suitcase, inside, brainstorm.* Together, sort the words into piles by rules of your child's choice, such as by initial consonant.

Day 5

This week your child is learning about characters, setting, and plot. As you read this week, talk together about how the characters and setting change as the story moves from beginning to middle to end.

4　　1

Two Words Make One

Materials paper, marker, scissors, paper clip, pencil, 1 button per player

Game Directions

1. Make a simple spinner as shown.

2. Players place buttons on Start, take turns spinning, and move the number of spaces shown.

3. When a player lands on a picture square, he or she must say the compound word that names the picture. Answers are shown below.

4. The first player to reach End wins!

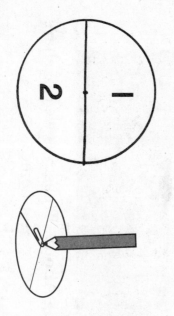

Answers (in order): football, eggshell, rainbow, cowboy, rowboat, cupcake, basketball, pinecone, snowflake

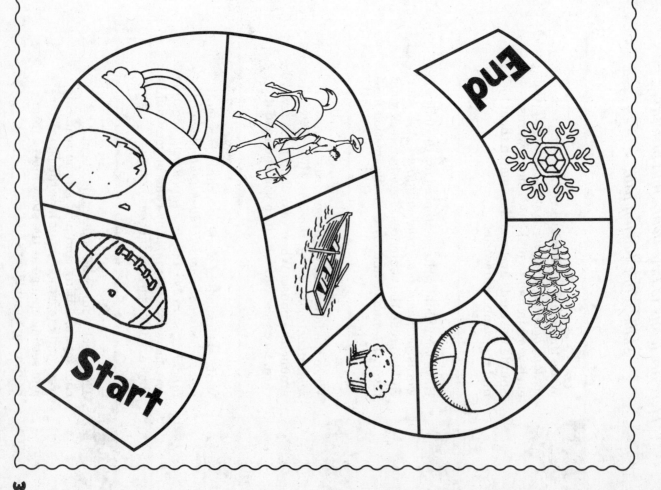

Name _____

Pick a word from the box to finish each compound word.

Write it on the line.

Draw a line to the picture it matches.

flashlight

| boat man paper watch |

_____
- -
1. news _____

_____
- -
2. row _____

_____
- -
3. wrist _____

_____
- -
4. snow _____

_____

Find the compound word.

Mark the ⬭ to show your answer.

5. ⬭ raining

⬭ rainy

⬭ raincoat

6. ⬭ mitten

⬭ marching

⬭ backpack

School + Home **Home Activity** Your child read compound words—words formed by joining two or more words. Have your child tell what two words make up these compound words: *rainbow, snowflake, peanut, baseball,* and *backpack.*

© Pearson Education 1

Name _____

Read the story.

Keesha was surprised to see a box in the hall.
Keesha thought, "What is in the box?
Is there treasure in the box?"
"Purr! Purr!" Keesha heard.
She looked in the box to find a surprise.
Ten kittens were in the box! Here comes their mom!

Circle the word or words that tell whom the story is about.

1. Keesha   a mother cat   a dog

Circle the word or words that tell where the story happens.

2. in the box   in the hall   in the treasure chest

Write 1, 2, 3 on the lines to tell what happens in the beginning, middle, and end.

3. _____ Keesha looks in the box.

4. _____ Mother cat comes for her kittens.

5. _____ Keesha sees a box in the hall.

© Pearson Education 1

Home Activity Your child identified the main character of a story, where the story took place, and the order of important events of a story. Ask your child to identify these things in the books that you read together.

104 **Comprehension** Character, Setting, and Plot   **Practice Book Unit 4**

Name _____

Circle the word for each picture.

S**ue** gr**ew** this fr**ui**t.

1.

blew   black

2.

flow   flew

3.

glue   glow

4.

chick   chew

5.

sit   suit

6.

stew   stop

7.

joke   juice

8.

news   nose

Find the word that has the same vowel sound as  .

9. ⬭ bruise
⬭ breeze
⬭ brass

10. ⬭ tree
⬭ true
⬭ try

© Pearson Education 1

 School + Home | **Home Activity** Your child practiced reading words with *ew, ue,* and *ui* as in *Sue, grew,* and *fruit.* Work with your child to make up silly rhyming pairs that contain this vowel sound and these spellings, such as *blue stew* or *fruit suit.*

Name _____

Pick a word from the box to finish each sentence.
Write it on the line.

picture   remember   room   stood   thought

_____
- - - - - - - - - - - - - - - - - - - -
1. Mom took a _____ of my friends and me.

_____
- - - - - - - - - - - - - - - - -
2. We _____ by a tree.

_____
- - - - - - - - - - - - - - - - -
3. I _____ the picture was wonderful.

_____
- -
4. I will hang the picture in my _____ .

_____
- -
5. It will help me _____ my friends.

Home Activity Your child learned to read the words *picture*, *remember*, *room*, *stood*, and *thought*. Write each word on a small piece of paper. Say each word. Have your child put the words in the order in which you read them and then repeat the words in a different order.

Practice Book Unit 4

Name _____

Pick a word from the box to finish each sentence.
Write it on the line.

> idea   picture   remember
> room   stood   thought

_____

1. I _____ my funny dream I had last night.

_____

2. I was in a _____ with a long curtain.
   Then, a crocodile came and ate all my biscuits!

_____

3. I _____ up and looked in a cradle.

_____

4. It had a _____ of a baby crocodile eating cookies!

_____

5. I woke up and _____ , "That dream was odd."

_____

6. I have no _____ what the dream means.

Home Activity Your child learned to read the words *biscuits, cookies, cradle, crocodile, curtain, idea, picture, remember, room, stood,* and *thought.* Write sentences leaving out these words. Have your child supply the missing word.

© Pearson Education 1

Name _____

Pick a word from the box to finish each sentence.
Write it on the line.

bright	high	lie
light	sight	

I eat p**ie** at n**igh**t.

_____
----
1. The moon is _____ in the sky.

_____
----
2. These give off _____ .

_____
----
3. They are a pretty _____ .

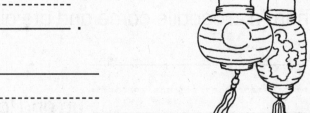

_____
----
4. We _____ on the grass and look up.

_____
----
5. It is a _____ fall night.

Home Activity Your child reviewed words with the long *i* sound spelled *ie* as in *pie* and *igh* as in *night*. Read the long *i* words on this page aloud. Ask your child to say a word that rhymes with each.

108 **Phonics** Long *i: ie, igh* Review

© Pearson Education 1

Name _____

Pick a word from the box to finish each sentence.
Write the words in the puzzles.

knees   knight   know
wreath   wren

1. They march with their _____ high.

2. I see a _____ on that float.

3. A _____ is on the float.

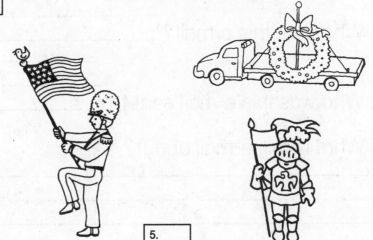

4. I _____ the song the band
is playing.

5. A _____ sits on the flagpole.

© Pearson Education 1

Home Activity Your child practiced reading words that begin with *kn* as in *knight* and *wr* as in *wrench*. Have your child draw pictures of *knee, knight, wrecker,* and *wren* and label each picture.

Name _____

Read the e-mail.
Answer the questions.

From: Alex
Subject: Going to the park
Date: April 4
To: Tom

I am going to the park at 3:00 today.
Do you want to come too? I'll be by the swings.

See you later,
Alex

1. Who sent this e-mail? _____

2. Who was this e-mail sent to? _____

3. What is this e-mail about?

_____

_____

4. When was this e-mail sent?

_____

_____

School + Home **Home Activity** Your child learned how to write, send, and reply to an e-mail. If possible, help your child compose and send an e-mail to a family member.

Family Times

You are your child's first and best teacher!

Name _____

This week we're

Reading Henry and Mudge and Mrs. Hopper's House

by Cynthia Rylant

Illustrated by Carolyn Brocken
in the style of Sucie Stevenson

160

161

*What will Henry and Mudge
find at Mrs. Hopper's house?*

Talking About Treasures we can share
with neighbors

Learning About Suffixes -ly, -ful
Vowels in moon
Cause and Effect

---

*Here are ways to help your child practice
skills while having fun!*

Day 1

Write the following words on cards: *hope, hopeful, thank, thankful, use, useful, slow, slowly, nice, nicely, wise, wisely.* Together, sort the words into word pairs.

Day 2

Write each word on a card: *moon, spoon, soon, tune, June, dune.* Have your child read the words and sort the cards by vowel patterns.

Day 3

Write the following words in a list: *across, because, dance, only, opened, shoes, told.* Together, write a short story that uses all the words. Illustrate a part of the story.

Day 4

Write each spelling word on a card: *slowly, careful, quickly, useful, painful, playful, sadly, gladly, nicely, wonderful.* Take turns reading and spelling a word. Then name a person or thing the word describes.

Day 5

This week your child is learning the difference between cause and effect. Discuss an event in the news and its cause or effect.

Add a Suffix

Materials paper, paper clip, scissors, pencil, marker, 1 button per player

Game Directions

1. Make a simple spinner as shown. Players place buttons on Start.

2. Take turns spinning. Move forward that number of spaces on the game board.

3. Read the word in the space. Write the word created by adding -*ly* or -*ful* to that word. If correct, player stays on the space. If incorrect, player goes back one space. Play continues until all players reach End.

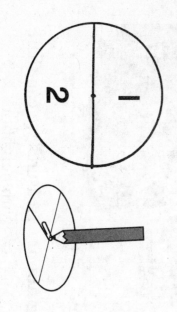

Answers: nightly, prideful, slowly, sadly, hopeful, restful, slowly, sadly, hopeful, gladly, playful, bravely, careful, nicely, graceful, softly, thankful

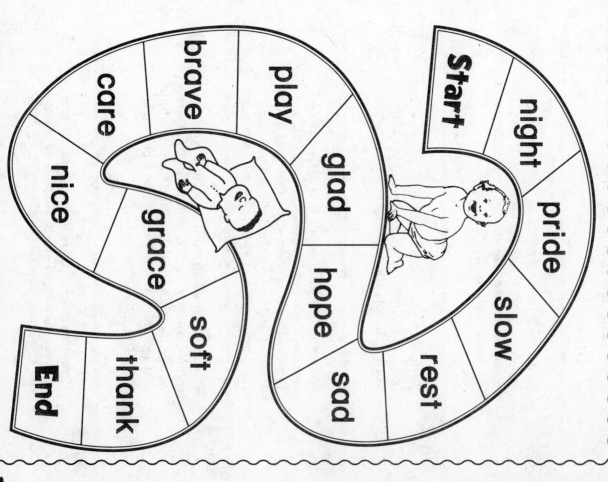

Start

night

pride

slow

rest

sad

hope

glad

play

brave

care

nice

grace

soft

thank

End

Name _____

Henry and Mudge

Add -ly or -**ful** to the word in ( ).
Write the new word on the line.

nice + -ly = nice**ly**

(play)

_____

- - - - - - - - - - - - - - -

1. The dog is _____ .

(slow)

_____

- - - - - - - - - - - - - - -

2. The dog walked _____ .

(quick)

_____

- - - - - - - - - - - - - - -

3. Then it ran _____ !

(safe)

_____

- - - - - - - - - - - - - - -

4. The dog got home _____ .

(thank)

_____

- - - - - - - - - - - - - - -

5. Miss Moon was _____ .

© Pearson Education 1

Home Activity Your child added -ly and -ful to words. Ask your child to give you instructions using words with the -ly suffix, such as *Clap loudly; Talk softly; Walk quickly.* Follow the instructions. Then have your child write simple sentences using *playful* and *thankful.*

Practice Book Unit 4

Phonics Suffixes -ly, -ful **113**

Name _____

Draw a line to match what happens with why it happens.

What Happens	**Why It Happens**

1.

2.

3.

4.

5.

© Pearson Education 1

 School + Home **Home Activity** Your child learned about what happens (effect) and why it happens (cause). While watching a sporting event, such as a soccer game or swim meet, invite your child to identify what happens and why.

Name _____

Circle the word for each picture.

 m<u>oo</u>n

---

1. 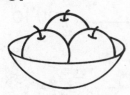	2. 	3. 	4.
zoo zip	span spoon	pal pool	stool stale

---

5. 	6. 	7. 	8.
fruit fool	gaze goose	boot bait	spool spill

Draw a picture for each word.

9. food

10. broom

 School + Home

Home Activity Your child practiced reading words with *oo* as in *moon*. Write the *oo* words from this page on scraps of paper. Have your child pick a word and use it in a sentence.

Name _____

Pick a word from the box to match each clue.
Write it on the line.

| across   because   dance   only   opened   shoes   told |

1.

_____

_____

2.

_____

_____

3.

_____

_____

4. She said, "I _____ you to read slowly."

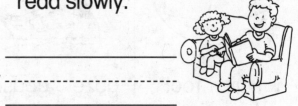

_____

_____

---

5. The plant grows _____ it has water.

_____

_____

6. Mom said, "_____ one treat!"

_____

_____

7.

_____

_____

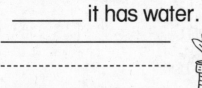

© Pearson Education 1

Practice Book Unit 4

Name _____

Pick a word from the box to finish each sentence.
Write it on the line.

> across   because   dance
> only   opened   shoes   told

_____

1. We had a party _____ it was Valentine's Day.

2. There were many hearts but _____ one gargoyle on the wall.

3. I like to _____ the waltz.

4. I dance _____ the room in my tuxedo.

5. Do you like my shiny dance _____ ?

6. She _____ the box and smiled.

7. My friend _____ me she liked my gift.

 Home Activity Your child learned to read the words *across, because, dance, gargoyle, heart, only, opened, shiny, shoes, told, tuxedo, Valentine's Day*, and *waltz*. Ask your child to point to each word and use it in a spoken sentence.

© Pearson Education 1

Name _____

Circle the compound word in each sentence.

---

1. Sue is Luis's babysitter.

2. Sue has a ponytail.

3. Luis and Sue play in the backyard.

4. They go in at sunset.

5. Luis does his homework.

6. Sue said, "It is bedtime."

7. Luis gets his toothbrush.

8. Mom parks in the driveway.

Find the compound word.
Mark the ⬭ to show your answer.

9. ⬭ tasteful
   ⬭ teaching
   ⬭ teacup

10. ⬭ campfire
    ⬭ camping
    ⬭ camped

Home Activity Your child reviewed compound words—words formed by joining two or more words. Have your child write each circled word and then draw a line dividing it into the two words that formed the compound (baby/sitter).

© Pearson Education 1

Name _____

Read the name of each pet below.
Pick words from the box with vowel sounds
that are spelled the same.
Write the words on the lines.

clue   cruise   due   few   fruit   grew   knew   true

Mew

1. _____

2. _____

3. _____

Juicy

4. _____

5. _____

Blue

6. _____

7. _____

8. _____

School + Home **Home Activity** Your child reviewed words with the vowel patterns *ew, ue,* and *ui.* Have your child write each word above again and circle the letters that stand for the vowel sound.

Name _____

Put each group of last names in ABC order.
Write the names on the lines.

> Turza   Taylor   Terry   Till

1. _____   3. _____

2. _____   4. _____

> Lin   Lewis   Lopez   Lance

5. _____   7. _____

6. _____   8. _____

> Costello   Clifton   Cruz   Chang

9. _____   11. _____

10. _____   12. _____

School + Home

Home Activity Your child learned to use alphabetical order to find names in a phone book. The next time you need a phone number, ask your child to help you find the information.

Name

Family Times

You are your child's first and best teacher!

This week we're

Reading Tippy-Toe Chick, Go!

Tippy-Toe Chick, GO!

What great idea will Little Chick have?

by George Shannon
Illustrated by Laura Dronzek

Talking About When a problem needs a clever solution

Learning About Diphthong *ow/ou/*
Syllables C + *le*
Character, Setting, and Plot

Here are ways to help your child practice skills while having fun!

Day 1

Together, think of rhyming words for the following: *clown* and *plow*. Examples: *down, gown, town, brown, frown; bow, cow, how, now, chow*. Write and read the words together.

Day 2

Make up a simple crossword or word search puzzle using the following words that your child is learning to read: *circle, cattle, middle, apple, candle*.

Day 3

Write the following words: *along, behind, eyes, never, pulling, toward*. Ask your child to read the words and then use them to make up an exciting story about a hero who saves someone.

Day 4

List the spelling words on paper: *how, town, down, now, brown, cow, clown, frown, crowd, growl*. Have your child copy each word, writing the *ow* in red and the remaining letters in blue.

Day 5

This week your child is learning about characters, setting, and plot. As you read together, talk about how the characters and setting change as the story moves from beginning to middle to end.

Brown Cow

Materials crayons

Game Directions

1. Players take turns reading the words on the page.

2. If the word has *ow* sound as in *cow*, the player colors the space brown.

3. If the word has a *ow* sound as in *row*, the player colors the space green.

4. Color the spaces for all other words blue.

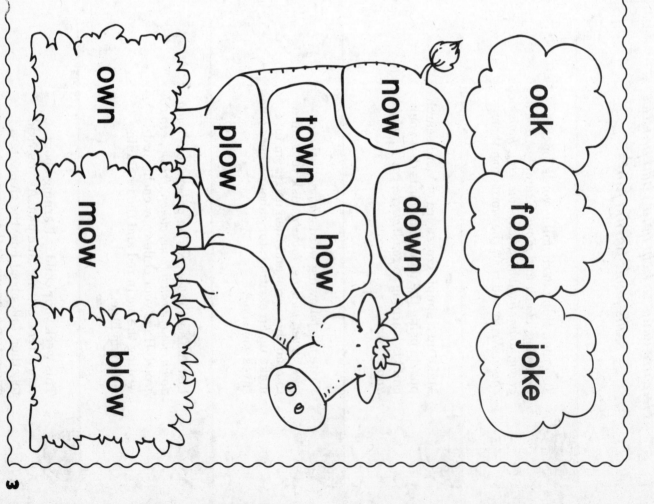

own | mow | blow

plow | town | how

now | down

oak | food | joke

Name _____

Pick a word from the box to match each picture.
Write it on the line.

cr**ow**n

| clown cow flower owl towel town |

1.

_____

- - - - - - - - - - - - - - - - - - -

_____

2.

_____

- - - - - - - - - - - - - - - - - - -

_____

3.

_____

- - - - - - - - - - - - - - - - - - -

_____

4.

_____

- - - - - - - - - - - - - - - - - - -

_____

5.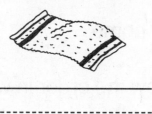

_____

- - - - - - - - - - - - - - - - - - -

_____

6.

_____

- - - - - - - - - - - - - - - - - - -

_____

Find the word that has the same vowel sound as .
Mark the ⬭ to show your answer.

7. ⬭ groom
   ⬭ grew
   ⬭ growl

8. ⬭ dune
   ⬭ down
   ⬭ den

Home Activity Your child read and wrote words with *ow* that have the vowel sound heard in *crown*.
Encourage your child to make a list of other words with *ow* that rhyme with *cow* and *brown*.

© Pearson Education 1

Name _____

Read the story.
Follow the directions.

Juan stared up at the tree. His kite was on a branch.
Juan thought, "How do **I** get the kite down?
That tree is very tall."
Juan saw a ball on the ground.
He gently tossed the ball high into the branches.
Down came the ball! Down sailed his kite.

Circle the word or words that tell who the story is about.

I. a kite

Juan

a tree

Circle the words that tell where the story happens.

2. by a tree

in a school

in a home

Number the sentences from 1 to 3 to show the order in which the events happened.

3. _____ Juan throws a ball at the kite.

4. _____ Juan's kite gets stuck in a tree.

5. _____ Juan's kite comes loose.

Home Activity This week your child identified who is in a story, where it takes place, and the important events of a story in the order in which they occurred. As you read together this week, ask your child to tell you who the story is about, where it takes place, and what happens in the story.

© Pearson Education 1

Circle the word for each picture.

bott**le**

1.	2.	3.	4.

cattle canned	tabbed table	picking pickle	turtle turned

5.	6.	7.	8.

candle candy	needy needle	handy handle	saddle sadder

Find the word that has the same ending sound as .
Mark the ⏝ to show your answer.

9. ⏝ litter
⏝ lightly
⏝ little

10. ⏝ purple
⏝ purred
⏝ purest

 School + Home **Home Activity** Your child read two-syllable words with *le* in the second syllable. Have your child fold a piece of paper into four boxes, choose four of the words he or she circled, find a rhyming word for that word, and draw pictures of the rhyming word. Ask your child to label each picture.

© Pearson Education 1

Name _____

Pick a word from the box to finish each sentence. **Write** it on the line. **Remember** to use a capital letter at the beginning of a sentence.

> along   behind   eyes   never   pulled   toward

1. The dogs walked _____ the wall.

2. The dogs stopped _____ the puddle.

3. Mom _____ the boy away.

4. _____ pet a dog you do not know well.

5. The puppy ran _____ its mother.

6. Its _____ were happy and bright.

Home Activity Your child learned to read the words *along, behind, eyes, never, pulled,* and *toward*. Ask your child to make up a puppet show using this week's words. Write out the script that your child dictates. Use paper bag or stick puppets to act it out.

© Pearson Education 1

Name _____

Pick a word from the box to finish each sentence. **Write** it on the line.
Remember to use a capital letter at the beginning of a sentence.

| along behind disagreed eyes |
| never pulled toward |

_____

1. Lacy and I looked _____ the rock for bugs.

_____

2. We _____ about our favorite bugs.

_____

3. _____ touch a strange bug.

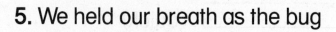

4. Then we found a potato bug

_____

with big _____ .
Our favorite!

5. We held our breath as the bug

_____

_____ a leaf behind it.

6. It pulled the leaf _____ a hole.

_____

7. We stood on tippy-toe to watch it crawl _____ the branch.

Home Activity Your child learned to read the words *along, behind, breath, disagreed, eyes, favorite, never, potato bugs, pulled, tippy-toe,* and *toward.* Ask your child to use each word in a spoken sentence.

© Pearson Education 1

Name _____

Read each sentence.

Add -ly or -ful to the word in ( ).

Write the new word on the line to finish each sentence.

1. The band started _____ . (sudden)

2. It was a _____ song! (wonder)

3. The band marched _____ . (quick)

4. Be _____ where you step. (care)

5. The girl sang _____ . (sweet)

Home Activity Your child reviewed adding -ly and -ful to words. Have your child tell a story about going somewhere with your family and use each word above.

128 **Phonics** Suffixes -ly, -ful Review

Name _____

Read each sentence.
Circle the word that has the same
vowel sound as **moon**.

m**oo**n

1. I eat lunch at noon.

2. Jamal puts a scoop of oats in my stall.

3. I don't eat with a spoon!

4. I like Jamal to groom me.

5. We go to the pool for a drink.

© Pearson Education 1

Home Activity Your child identified words with the same vowel sound as *moon*. Help your child write a
short poem using words that rhyme with *moon* and *pool*.

Practice Book Unit 5   **Phonics** Vowels in *moon* Review   **129**

Name _____

Read the sentences.

Birds don't want other animals to eat their chicks. Mother birds keep their babies safe. Some birds lay eggs that look like rocks. Other birds have chicks that are the same color as the ground. These are two ways that keep other animals from hurting the babies.

Write notes about what you learned.

1. Birds do not want _____

_____ .

2. Some eggs look _____ .

3. Some chicks' feathers are _____

_____ .

School + Home **Home Activity** Your child learned how to read a resource to take notes. Read an article with your child; help your child take notes on the important parts.

Family Times

You are your child's first and best teacher!

This week we're

Reading Mole and the Baby Bird

Talking About How new ideas can help us see things differently

Learning About Diphthong ou/ou/
Syllables VCV
Sequence of Events

Here are ways to help your child practice skills while having fun!

Day 1

Write a note together to family members, using as many *ou* words as possible. Some words you might use are: *hour, sound, ourselves, outdoors, found, outside, about, around, amount, count.*

Day 2

Read these two-syllable words with your child: *river, bacon, cabin, camel, lemon, pilot, wagon tiger, decoy.* Together, read them again and clap out the syllables.

Day 3

Encourage your child to write sentences that include the following new words: *door, loved, should, wood.*

Day 4

Dictate the following spelling words and have your child write them: *mouth, house, found, our, out, cloud, ouch, shout, round, count.* Then have your child underline the *ou* in each word.

Day 5

This week your child is learning about the order in which events occur in a story. As you read together this week, have your child tell what happened first, next, and last in the story.

Spin and Spell

Materials paper, scissors, paper clip, pencil, 1 button per player

Game Directions

1. Make a simple spinner as shown.

2. Players take turns spinning and then naming and spelling a word with the *ou* sound as in *out* and *cow.* Possible words: *our, sound, about, round, scout, loud, cloud, count, trout, out, ouch, down, town, brown, how, now, cow, plow, growl.*

3. If the word is spelled correctly, the player may move that number of spaces as shown on the spinner.

4. Play continues until all players reach End.

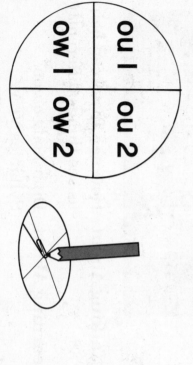

ou 1	ou 2
ow 1	ow 2

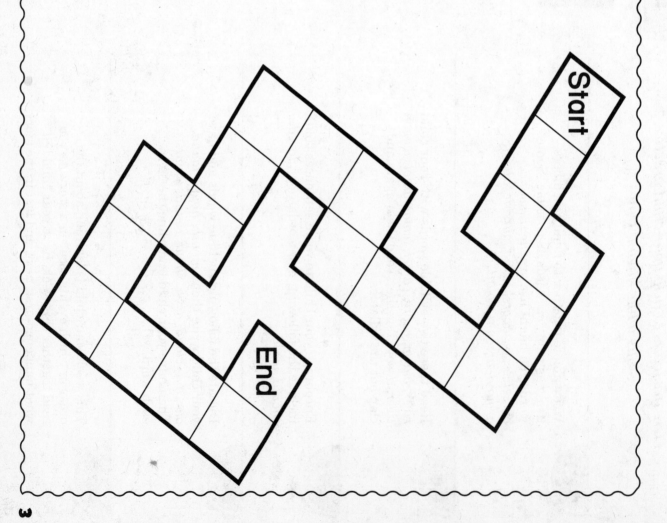

Start

End

Name _____

Write a word from the box
to match each picture.

| couch | flour | hound |
| house | mouse | spout |

1.

_____
- - - - - - - - - - - - - - - -

2.

_____
- - - - - - - - - - - - - - - -

3.

_____
- - - - - - - - - - - - - - - -

4.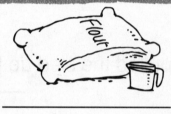

_____
- - - - - - - - - - - - - - - -

5.

_____
- - - - - - - - - - - - - - - -

6.

_____
- - - - - - - - - - - - - - - -

Find the word that has the same vowel sound as .
Mark the ⬭ to show your answer.

7. ⬭ sand
   ⬭ sound
   ⬭ send

8. ⬭ sheet
   ⬭ shut
   ⬭ shout

Home Activity Your child read and wrote words with *ou* that have the vowel sound heard in *cloud*. Encourage your child to make a list of other words with *ou* that rhyme with *found* and *shout*.

Practice Book Unit 5   **Phonics** Vowel Diphthong ou/ou/   **133**

Name _____

Look at the pictures.
Write 1, 2, 3 to put the sentences in order.

_____

1. The sled flew down the hill. _____

_____

2. We pulled the sled up the hill. _____

_____

3. We sat on the sled. _____

_____

4. We will go out on the stage. _____

_____

5. We will put on our dance shoes. _____

_____

6. We will bow as the people clap. _____

© Pearson Education 1

Home Activity Your child put events in order to form a story. Ask your child to draw a series of pictures showing three events in the order in which they happened.

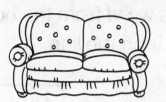

Circle the word for each picture.

 s<u>ofa</u>

---

1. 	2.	3. 	4.
lesson lemon	pillow pilot	bacon basket	wagging wagon

---

5. 	6.	7. 	8. 
river rigged	napkin navel	timber tiger	came camel

Draw a picture for each word.

9. spider

10. shadow

 Home Activity Your child read words with two syllables that have one consonant in the middle. Have your child choose five words from the page and use each word in a sentence.

Name _____

Pick a word from the box to finish each sentence.
Write it on the line.

<pre>
    door   loved   should   wood
</pre>

Dear Jack,

I had such a good time at your house last week.

_____

I _____ it when we played in the snow!

Remember when we made an igloo?

_____

We used a blanket for the _____, and it froze stiff.

_____

You _____ come to my house!

It is very warm here even in the winter.

_____

My dad and I are going to paint the _____ rail.

     Your friend,

     Sam

Home Activity Your child learned to read the words *door, loved, should,* and *wood*. Ask your child to write a story that uses each word and read it aloud.

Pick a word from the box to match each clue.
Write it on the line.

borrowed   door   loved   presently
should   usually   wood

I.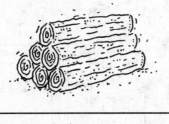

_____

- - - - - - - - - - - - - - - -

_____

2.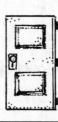

_____

- - - - - - - - - - - - - - - -

_____

3. You _____ say, "Thank you."

_____

- - - - - - - - - - - - - - - -

_____

4. after a little time passes

_____

- - - - - - - - - - - - - - - -

_____

5. most of the time

_____

- - - - - - - - - - - - - - - -

_____

6. I liked it a lot! I _____ it.

_____

- - - - - - - - - - - - - - - -

_____

_____

- - - - - - - - - - - - - - - -

7. I do not own this. I _____ it.

 Home Activity Your child learned to read the words *borrowed, door, loved, presently, should, usually,* and *wood.* Draw a curved line to look like a path. Write the words from this page along the path. Have your child read the words while "traveling" the path.

Name _____

Read each sentence.
Circle the word that has the same vowel sound as **crown**.

cr<u>ow</u>n

1. Mr. Hill walked downtown.

2. He saw a brown dog.

3. Mr. Hill frowned.

4. How could he help the dog?

5. Mr. Hill looked down at the tag.
   Now he knew what to do!

© Pearson Education 1

Home Activity Your child identified words with the same vowel sound as *crown*. Ask your child to write a short poem using words that rhyme with *how* and *brown*.

Name _____

Pick a word from the box to match each clue.
Write the words in the puzzles.

> candle   little   middle   needle   purple   uncle

1. red + blue =

2. not aunt

3. something sharp

4. halfway

5. not big

6. gives off light

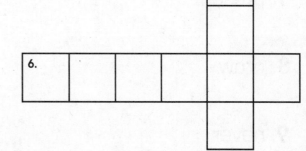

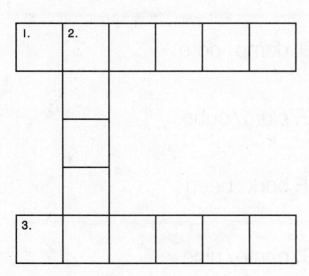

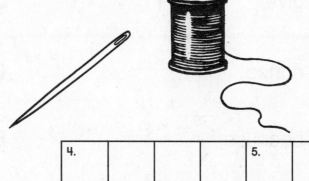

© Pearson Education 1

Home Activity Your child solved puzzles using two-syllable words with a consonant and *le* in the second syllable. Make up your own crossword puzzle with clues using two-syllable words with a consonant and *le* as the second syllable. Then have your child do the puzzle.

Name _____

Read the numbered words in each list.
Match each numbered word with the guide words that show where you would find the word in a dictionary.
Draw a line from the numbered word to its guide words.

1. mouth   A. part / plant

2. picture   B. gerbil / goose

3. give   C. mouse / much

4. dance   D. damp / date

5. because   E. clam / cube

6. color   F. bark / beep

7. present   G. name / nice

8. draw   H. dish / duck

9. never   I. porch / price

Home Activity Your child learned about using alphabetical order and guide words in a dictionary. Help your child look up other words in a dictionary at home.

Name

Family Times

You are your child's first and best teacher!

This week we're

Reading Dot & Jabber and
the Great Acorn Mystery

*How will Dot and Jabber
solve this mystery?*

Dot & Jabber
and the Great Acorn Mystery

by Ellen Stoll Walsh

Talking About Why we want to find
answers to some questions

Learning About Vowels in *book*
Inflected Endings
Compare and Contrast

---

*Here are ways to help your child practice
skills while having fun!*

Day 1

Say one of the following words and have your
child think of two words that rhyme with it:
look and *stood* (*book, shook, wood, good*).

Day 2

Write these words: *liked, waving, voting,
hopes, fixes, smiling*. Have your child write the
base word for each word. Help with spelling
changes, if needed.

Day 3

Write the following words in a list: *among,
another, instead, none*. Together, write a poem
about spending the day with friends or about
a happy day spent alone.

Day 4

Write each spelling word on a card: *book,
moon, took, food, look, pool, zoo, noon, good,
foot*. Have your child sort the words into two
groups, according to vowel sounds.

Day 5

This week your child is learning how things
in a story are alike and different. As you read
this week, discuss ways in which things in
your story are alike and different.

Look at a Book

Materials index cards, marker, paper, 1 button for each player.

Game Directions

1. Fold 12 index cards in half to make a "book." Write one of the words from below on the outside "cover" of each. Write 1, 2, or 3 on the inside of each. Draw a game board, such as the one shown on p. 3.

2. Place the books in a small box or bag.

3. Players take turns picking one book from the box or bag. Each player reads aloud the word on the book cover and then moves the number of spaces written on the inside of the book.

4. Play continues until all players have reached End.

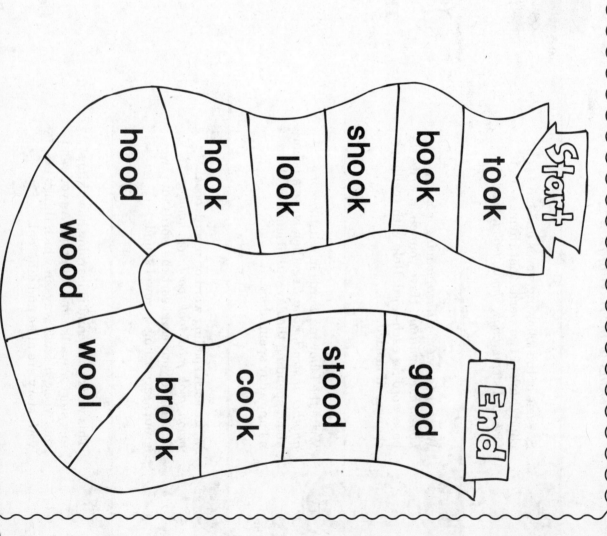

Took
2

Start — took — book — shook — look — hook — hood — wood — wool — brook — cook — stood — good — End

© Pearson Education 1

Circle the word for each picture.

b**oo**k

1.

had   hood

2.

cook   coat

3.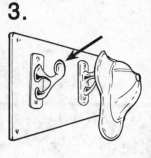

hook   hard

4.

wide   wood

5.

pooch   pouch

6.

look   lock

7.

store   stood

8.

brook   brake

Find the word that has the same vowel sound as  .
Mark the ⬭ to show your answer.

9. ⬭ tock
   ⬭ take
   ⬭ took

10. ⬭ greed
    ⬭ goat
    ⬭ good

Home Activity Your child read and wrote words with *oo* that have the vowel sound heard in *book*. Encourage your child to make lists that sort the words into those that rhyme with *took* and those that rhyme with *good*.

School + Home

© Pearson Education 1

Name _____

Look at the picture.
Circle the answer to each question.
Hint: One question will have two answers.

Nibbles   Whiskers

1. Who is big?   Nibbles   Whiskers

2. Who is little?   Nibbles   Whiskers

3. Who is sitting up?   Nibbles   Whiskers

4. Who is sleeping?   Nibbles   Whiskers

5. Who is a mouse?   Nibbles   Whiskers

6. **Draw** two trees that look the same.

7. **Draw** two trees that do not look the same.

© Pearson Education 1

Home Activity Your child compared and contrasted two animal characters. Choose two animals that your child likes. Have your child tell how the animals are alike and different.

Name _____

Add -**s**, -**ed**, or -**ing** to the word in ( ).
Write the new word on the line.

(hope + -s)

_____

----

1. Jean _____ to grow corn.

(slope + -ing)

_____

----

2. She plants seeds on the _____ hill.

(care + -ed)

_____

----

3. Jean _____ for the plants.

(taste + -ed)

_____

----

4. Jean _____ the corn.

(smile + -ing)

_____

----

5. She is _____ .

Home Activity Your child added -s, -ed, -ing to verbs that end in e. Write *hope, slope, care, rope,* and *smile* on a sheet of paper. Ask your child to tell the rule about adding -s, -ed, and -ing to each word. Then write the new words.

© Pearson Education 1

Name _____

Read the sentence. **Unscramble** the letters.
Write the word on the line. **Remember** to use
a capital letter at the beginning of a sentence.

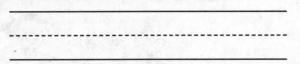

among   another   instead   none

1. I will have **ahernot**.

_____
- -
_____

2. **eNon** of the fruit is left.

_____
- -
_____

3. Eat this **ineadst**.

_____
- -
_____

4. He likes to nap **angmo** his dogs.

_____
- -
_____

 Home Activity Your child learned to read the words *among, another, instead,* and *none.* Write sentences such as these: *Is there another towel like this one? Try this one instead. None of the pie is left.* Leave a blank where the word should be, and have your child fill it in.

Name _____

Write a word from the box to finish each sentence.

> among another instead mystery none solve

1. We will be detectives today
   _____

   _____ of playing in the meadow.

   _____
   ----
2. What will we find _____ a million clues?

   _____
   ----
3. We want to solve a _____ .

   _____
   ----
4. Hey! Can you _____ the
   mystery of the missing food?

   _____
   ----
5. _____ of the clues are in the hall!

6. Hurray! Here is a clue.
   _____

   And here is _____ clue!

Home Activity Your child learned to read the words *among, another, detectives, hey, hurray, instead, meadow, million, mystery, none,* and *solved.* Write each word on a slip of paper. Scatter the papers around the house. Have your child find the words and read them to you.

Name _____

Pick a word from the box to match each picture.
Write it on the line.

h<u>ou</u>se

| blouse | bounce | cloud | pouch | scout | shout |

1.

_____
- - - - - - - - - - - - - - - - -
_____

2.

_____
- - - - - - - - - - - - - - - - -
_____

3.

_____
- - - - - - - - - - - - - - - - -
_____

4.

_____
- - - - - - - - - - - - - - - - -
_____

5.

_____
- - - - - - - - - - - - - - - - -
_____

6.

_____
- - - - - - - - - - - - - - - - -
_____

Home Activity Your child reviewed words with *ou* that have the vowel sound heard in *house*.
Encourage your child to use each word above in a sentence.

© Pearson Education 1

Name _____

Circle the word to finish each sentence.
Write the letter on the line.

mellon   melon

_____

- - - - - - - - - - - - - - -

1. Mom sliced a _____ .

salad   sallad

_____

- - - - - - - - - - - - - - -

2. Tina put a _____ on a plate.

lemons   lemmons

_____

- - - - - - - - - - - - - - -

3. Dad squeezed _____ .

baccon   bacon

_____

- - - - - - - - - - - - - - -

4. Now Dad cooks the _____ .

finish   finnish

_____

- - - - - - - - - - - - - - -

5. Soon we will _____ making lunch.

© Pearson Education 1

School + Home

Home Activity Your child completed words with two syllables that have one consonant in the middle. Name some foods you like. Ask your child to identify the middle consonant sounds in the words.

Practice Book Unit 5   **Phonics** Syllables VCV Review   **149**

Name _____

Look at the picture graph.
Answer the questions.

Our Favorite Animals

Number of People	Duck	Cat	Dog	Fish
7		🐱		
6		🐱	🐕	
5	🦆	🐱	🐕	
4	🦆	🐱	🐕	
3	🦆	🐱	🐕	🐟
2	🦆	🐱	🐕	🐟
1	🦆	🐱	🐕	🐟

Duck   Cat   Dog   Fish

1. Which is the most favorite animal? _____

2. Which is the least favorite animal? _____

3. How many children like dogs best? _____

4. How many children like ducks? _____

Home Activity Your child learned how to read a picture graph. Help your child make a picture graph to represent the favorite foods of members of your family.

Name _____

Family Times

You are your child's first and best teacher!

This week we're

Reading Simple Machines

114 115

Talking About Great ideas that make our lives easier

Learning About Diphthongs *oi, oy*
Suffixes *-er, -or*
Main Idea

Here are ways to help your child practice skills while having fun!

Day 1

Together, write the following words in sentences: *enjoy, toy, point, voice, coin, noise.* Choose your favorite sentence to illustrate together.

Day 2

Write each word on a card: *painter, baker, shopper, jogger, actor, sailor, doctor.* Shuffle the cards. Take turns picking a card and acting out the "job" on the card for the other player to guess.

Day 3

Write the following words in a list: *against, goes, heavy, kinds, today.* Have your child read the words. Together, look for the words in a children's magazine or book.

Day 4

Write the spelling words in a list: *oil, soil, voice, point, boy, boil, coin, oink, toy, join.* With your child, practice writing the words with crayons and then illustrate the words.

Day 5

This week your child is learning about the main idea in a story. As you read together, discuss what the story was mostly about.

Make Some Noise

Materials 1 coin, 1 button per player

Game Directions

1. Players place buttons on Start.

2. Players take turns flipping the coin and moving one space for heads or two for tails.

3. Player reads aloud the word on the space. If the word contains the vowel sound heard in *noise* or *boy*, the player may flip and move again.

4. The first player to reach End wins!

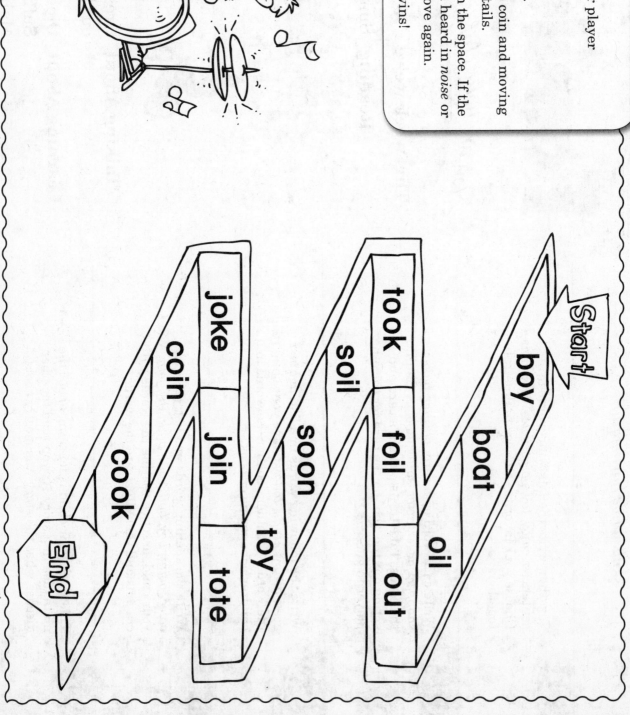

Start

boy boat oil

took foil out

soil soon toy

joke join tote

coin cook

End

Name _____

Circle the word for each picture.

 to<u>y</u>    s<u>oi</u>l

---

| 1.  coins   canes | 2.  bay   boy | 3.  boil   bail | 4.  joy   jay |

| 5.  boil   book | 6.  all   oil | 7.  foil   fail | 8.  round   royal |

Find the word that has the same vowel sound as **point**.
Mark the ⬭ to show your answer.

9. ⬭ join
⬭ jack
⬭ June

10. ⬭ spill
⬭ spoil
⬭ spout

 School + Home   **Home Activity** Your child read and wrote words with *oi* and *oy* heard in *toy* and *soil*. Have your child sort the *oi* and *oy* words on this page and make two lists. Then have him or her read the words aloud.

Name _____

Read each story.
Circle the words that tell what the story is about.
Draw a picture to show what the story is about.

---

1. People tripped on the stone.
   A wheelbarrow can move the stone.
   Now the walk is safe.

   making the walk safe
   tripping on stones
   moving stones

2.

---

3. A man can use a vacuum to clean.
   The job will go fast.
   It will be done in no time at all.

   Vacuums save time.
   Cleaning is fun.
   People have lots of jobs.

4.

Write a title for this story.

5. Mike and Jake are mules.
   They pull carts of hay.
   They help with work.

   _____

   -

   _____

Home Activity Your child identified the main idea in a story. Read a story together sand encourage your child to tell you what the story is about in one or two sentences.

Name _____

Write a word from the box
to match each picture.

 work**er**

| baker | sailor | painter | teacher |

1.  _____

2. _____

3.  _____

4.  _____

Draw a picture of each word.

5. driver

6. actor

© Pearson Education 1

School + Home

Home Activity Your child read and wrote words that end in *-er* and *-or* as in *worker* and *actor*. Write each word on a slip of paper. Have your child draw a slip and act out the word for you to guess.

Name _____

Pick a word from the box to finish each sentence.
Write it in the puzzle.

against   goes   heavy   kind   today

1. We push the
umbrella _____ the wind.

2. The rain _____ into
our shoes.

3. This _____ of rain
makes big puddles!

4. Rain this _____ does
not happen often.

5. We will need
dry socks _____ !

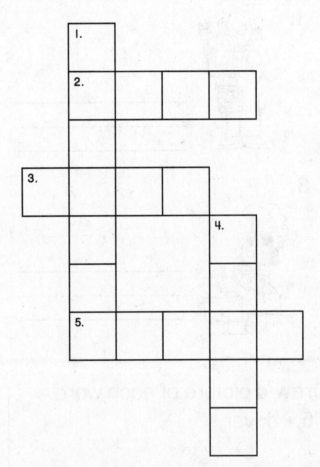

Home Activity Your child learned to read the words *against*, *goes*, *heavy*, *kind*, and *today*. Ask your child to use the words in a silly song. Write the words of the song and invite him or her to illustrate it.

Name _____

Pick a word from the box to finish each sentence. **Write** it on the line. **Remember** to use a capital letter at the beginning of a sentence.

> against   goes   heavy
> kind   machines   today

_____
----
1. _____ Bob and Joe found a box of pulleys, axles, and other parts.

_____
----
2. "We can make a toy with these _____!" Bob said.

_____
----
3. "What _____ of toy should we make?" asked Joe.

_____
----
4. The box was very _____ .

_____
----
5. They put a board _____ the table to make an inclined plane. They used a vacuum to clean the surface.

_____
----
6. "There _____ the box!" said Bob as the box slid onto the lawn.

 Home Activity Your child learned to read the words *against, axles, goes, heavy, inclined plane, kind, lawn, machines, pulleys, surface, today,* and *vacuum*. Invite your child to look for examples of each word and point them out as you go about your daily routines.

© Pearson Education 1

Name _____

Circle the word for each picture.
Write it on the line.

 w**oo**ds

---

1.

hack
hook
hike

_____
- - - - - - - - - - - - - - - - -
_____

2.

book
back
bike

_____
- - - - - - - - - - - - - - - - -
_____

3.

stone
steed
stood

_____
- - - - - - - - - - - - - - - - -
_____

4.

hide
hand
hood

_____
- - - - - - - - - - - - - - - - -
_____

5.

shook
shout
sheet

_____
- - - - - - - - - - - - - - - - -
_____

 School + Home

Home Activity Your child reviewed words with *oo* that have the vowel sound heard in *book*. Encourage your child to use pairs of words in silly sentences. Example: *I stood on a book and shook.*

Name _____

Add -s, -es, and **-ed** to each word.
Write the new word on the line.

	Add -s or -es	Add -ed
raise	1. _____	2. _____
hike	3. _____	4. _____

Add -ed and **-ing** to each word.
Write the new word on the line.

	Add -ed	Add -ing
use	5. _____	6. _____
save	7. _____	8. _____

Find the word that changes spelling when adding **-ing**.
Mark the ⬭ to show your answer.

9. ⬭ washing
   ⬭ waving
   ⬭ walking

10. ⬭ sharing
    ⬭ catching
    ⬭ singing

School + Home

Home Activity Your child added -s, -ed, and -ing to verbs that end in e. Have your child pick three words from above, draw a picture for each, and use each word in a sentence.

© Pearson Education 1

Name _____

Read the captions. **Match** the captions to the pictures.
Write the number of the caption on the line.

| 1. Cars can take you places. | 3. A ramp is a simple machine. |
| 2. A bike has two wheels. | 4. A pulley can lift a heavy weight. |

_ _ _ _ _ _ _ _
_____

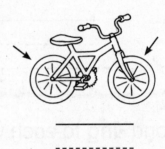

_ _ _ _ _ _ _ _
_____

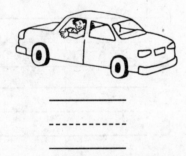

_ _ _ _ _ _ _ _
_____

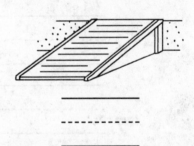

_ _ _ _ _ _ _ _
_____

Write a caption for this picture.

_____
_ _
5. _____

Home Activity Your child learned to match captions to the pictures to which they belong. Look at pictures in a book or newspaper with your child and have your child make up captions to match each picture.

Family Times

Name

You are your child's first and best teacher!

This week we're

Reading Alexander Graham Bell

Talking About How a great idea can change the way we live

Learning About Vowels *aw, au*
Short *e: ea*
Draw Conclusions

Here are ways to help your child practice skills while having fun!

Day 1

Ask your child to use the words *cause, sauce, slaw,* and *thaw* to write a short story about a delicious dinner.

Day 2

Write each word on a card: *head, ready, thread, weather, spread, feather, bread, steady.* Work with your child to sort the words into groups of words that rhyme.

Day 3

Write the following words in a list: *built, early, learn, science, through.* Have your child read the words. Then make up a sentence for each word. Leave a blank where the word belongs. Have your child fill in the missing word.

Day 4

Write each spelling word on a card: *saw, draw, crawl, straw, law, jaw, paw, lawn, yawn, hawk.* Have children write and illustrate each word. Check the spelling.

Day 5

This week your child is learning to draw conclusions based on the text as well as what he or she already knows. As you read, stop often and discuss what ideas the author may be communicating indirectly.

4

1

Aw, Au Match-Up

Materials paper, scissors, markers, 1 coin

Game Directions

1. Make picture cards like the ones shown. Make matching word cards.

2. Shuffle the cards and lay them out face down in a grid.

3. Players take turns flipping over two cards. If the word card matches the picture card, the player keeps the pair and tries again. If the cards do not match, the cards are flipped face down again, and play passes to the next player.

4. Play continues until all the cards are matched.

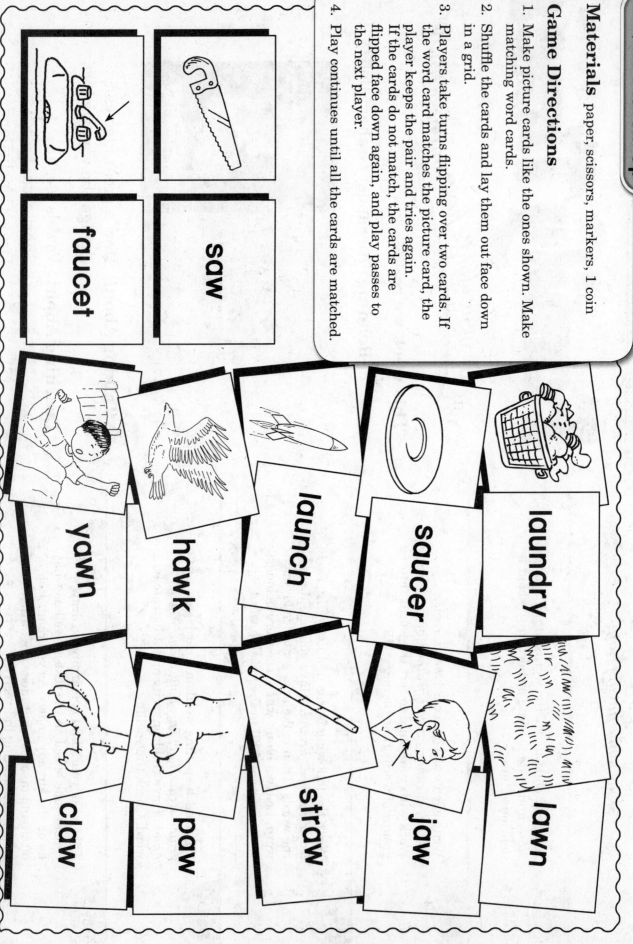

faucet

saw

yawn

hawk

launch

saucer

laundry

claw

paw

straw

jaw

lawn

Name _____

Circle the word for each picture.

 <u>sa</u>w    <u>au</u>to

1. 	**2.** 	**3.** 	**4.** 
pail paw	yawn yard	lunch launch	stray straw

5. 	**6.** 	**7.** 	**8.** 
false faucet	crawl call	lane lawn	laundry landed

Find the word that has the same vowel sound as .
Mark the ⬭ to show your answer.

9. ⬭ sash
   ⬭ sauce
   ⬭ such

10. ⬭ clay
    ⬭ clue
    ⬭ claw

 School + Home   **Home Activity** Your child read words with the vowels *aw* and *au* as heard in *saw* and *auto*. Have your child make silly rhyming sentences using words that rhyme with *saw*. Example: *The cat can draw with her paw.*

Name _____

Read the story.

Marty found coins on the ground. In fact, he found five dimes and three quarters. Marty felt rich! He picked up the coins and smiled. Marty started to walk away. He saw a girl sitting on a bench. She held a torn purse in her hands. She was crying.

Answer the questions.

1. Why do you think the girl is crying?

_____

_____

2. What kind of person do you think Marty is?

_____

_____

3. What do you think Marty will do?
   Draw a picture.

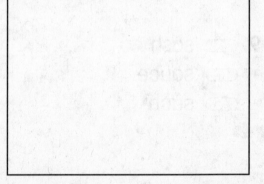

Home Activity Your child used what he or she already knew about a situation to draw conclusions about an event. Read through a book with your child. Have your child tell what he or she thinks about the main character.

Circle the word for each picture.

 br**ea**d

---

1.

head   had

2.

three   thread

3.

spray   spread

4.

feather   father

5.

tread   tree

6.

sweet   sweater

7.

watch   wealth

8.

lather   leather

Find the word that has the same **short e** sound as .
Mark the ⬭ to show your answer.

9. ⬭ study
    ⬭ sticky
    ⬭ steady

10. ⬭ health
    ⬭ hurt
    ⬭ heel

© Pearson Education 1

School + Home   **Home Activity** Your child read words in which the short e sound is spelled *ea*, as in *bread*. Have your child read aloud each word and use it in a sentence.

Name _____

Read the sentence.
Unscramble the letters.
Write the word on the line.

| built early learn science through |

1. Many boys and girls like **sciceen**. _____

2. We **lnear** about plants. _____

3. We get up **earyl** to see the _____

sun rise. _____

4. We **uiltb** a little car! _____

5. We look **ourghth** the glass. _____

© Pearson Education 1

Home Activity Your child learned to read the words *built, early, learn, science,* and *through*. Find children's books about famous scientists and mathematicians. Read them together and challenge your child to find the words in the text.

Name _____

Pick a word from the box to finish each sentence.
Write it on the line.

> built   early   learn   piano   science   through

1. The man who _____ the first telephone is famous.
He was born in Scotland. He was a teacher in Boston.

2. He wanted to _____ about everything.

3. He learned to play the _____ .

4. He used _____ to make machines. His machines
helped people to communicate.

5. He got up _____ and went to bed late.

6. He learned that electricity makes sound

travel _____ wires.

Home Activity Your child learned to read the words *Boston, built, communicate, early, electricity, famous, learn, piano, science, Scotland, telephone,* and *through*. Look for books about Alexander Graham Bell to read together. Encourage your child to use these words to tell you about this famous man.

Name _____

Write the word for each picture.

boil   toy   boy   oil

 joy

 co<u>i</u>ns

_____

- - - - - - - - - - - - - - -

1. Give the _____ to the _____.

_____

- - - - - - - - - - - - - - -

2. The _____ is going to _____.

Circle the words with the same vowel sound as .

3. Roy digs a hole in the soil.

4. Troy would like to join the team.

5. Give the foil to Joy.

 School + Home

Home Activity Your child reviewed words with *oy* and *oi* that have the vowel sound heard in *joy* and *coin*. Work with your child to write a short story using as many of the words on the page as possible.

© Pearson Education 1

Name _____

Pick a word from the box to match each clue.
Write the words in the puzzles.

baker   driver   painter   sailor   seller   worker

1. I paint.

2. I sail.

3. I bake.

4. I drive.

5. I sell.

6. I work.

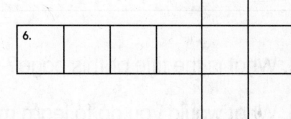

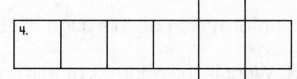

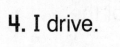© Pearson Education 1

School + Home **Home Activity** Your child reviewed words that end in *-er* and *-or*. Let your child choose three of the words to illustrate. Have your child describe each picture.

Practice Book Unit 5   **Phonics** Suffixes *-er, -or* Review   **169**

Name _____

Look at the Web page.
Answer the questions.

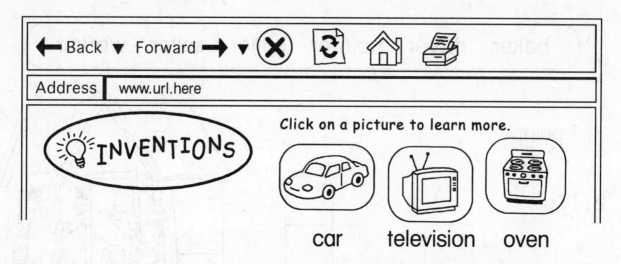

Click on a picture to learn more.

INVENTIONS

car   television   oven

1. Which button would you click on to look at the page you

    _____

    ----

    looked at before this one? _____

2. Which picture would you click on to make a copy of the

    _____

    ----

    information on this page? _____

3. What is the address of this page?

    _____

    _____

    _____

    ----

4. What is the title of this page? _____

5. What would you do to learn more about ovens?

    _____

    _____

© Pearson Education 1

School + Home **Home Activity** Your child learned about using a Web page to find information. When you and your child are online, discuss how to navigate the Web.

Family Times

Name

You are your child's first and best teacher!

This week we're

Reading Ben Franklin and His First Kite

Talking About How you can use something familiar in a new way

Learning About Prefixes *un-*, *re-*
Long Vowels *i, o*
Theme

Here are ways to help your child practice skills while having fun!

Day 1
Write the following words in a list: *rewrite, repaint, repay, unhappy, untie, unfold*. Read the list together and talk about what kind of action or idea each word describes.

Day 2
Write these word parts on a card: *ost, old, ind,* and *ild*. Take turns picking a card and thinking of a word that rhymes with that word part. Answers could include: *most, post, fold, mold, find, kind, mild, wild*.

Day 3
Write the following words in a list: *answered, brothers, carry, different, poor*. Together, write and read sentences using the words.

Day 4
Write the spelling words in a list: *unhappy, refill, untie, undo, repay, unkind, undress, retell, reopen, refund*. Have students copy each word on a card or small piece of paper and sort the words according to prefixes.

Day 5
This week your child is learning about the theme, or the big idea, in a story. As you read together this week, stop and discuss the big idea of the story.

Spin and Spell

Materials paper, scissors, paper clip, pencil,
1 button per player

Game Directions

1. Make a simple spinner as shown.
2. Players take turns spinning and moving their
   buttons the number of spaces shown.
3. Each player reads aloud the word on the space
   and then adds *un-* or *re-* to the front of the word
   to make a new word. The word must be a real
   word. If the player cannot think of a real word,
   then the player must move back one space.
4. The first player to reach END wins!

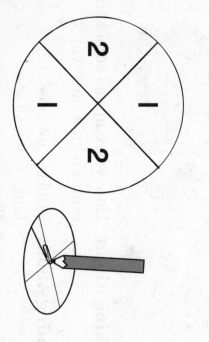

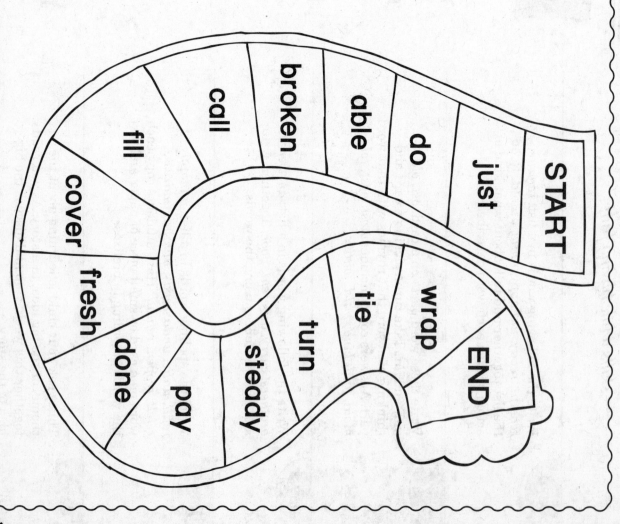

Name _____

Add re- or un- to the word in ( ).
Write the new word on the line.

re- + do = **re**do
un- + clear = **un**clear

(build)

_____

1. Mr. Ford will _____ the car.

(happy)

_____

2. He is _____ with the color.

(paint)

_____

3. He will _____ it.

(fills)

_____

4. He _____ the car with gas.

(lock)

_____

5. Don't forget to _____ the door!

School + Home
Home Activity Your child added the prefixes *un-* and *re-* to words. Ask your child to think of other words to which *un-* and *re-* can be added. Have them list the words and use them in sentences.

Name _____

Read the story.
Follow the directions below.

It is time to work!
I rake the leaves.
You sweep the sidewalk.
We work hard.
Now the work is done. We can play!

I. Which sentence below tells the big idea? **Underline** it.
   We must work before we play.
   It is time to sweep.
   It is hard to rake the lawn.

2.–4. How did you know the big idea? **Underline** three
      sentences in the story that helped you know.

5. **Draw** a picture to show what work you do.

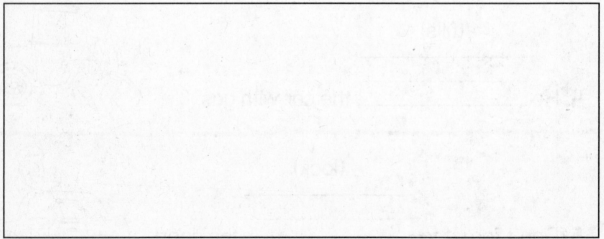

Home Activity Your child identified a story's theme or its big idea. Read a story with your child. Discuss the
story's big idea together and connect this idea to something in your child's life.

© Pearson Education 1

Name _____

Circle the word for each picture.

 p**ost**    g**old**    **rind**    **wild**

1. 	**2.** 	**3.** 	**4.** 
fold fell	kite kind	child chilled	mast most

5. 	**6.** 	**7.**	**8.** 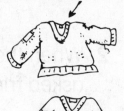
cold call	fin find	wind went	old all

Find the word that has the **long o** sound.
Mark the ⬭ to show your answer.

9. ⬭ told
     ⬭ tall
     ⬭ tied

10. ⬭ house
      ⬭ heat
      ⬭ host

School + Home

Home Activity Your child read words with the long *o* sound as in *post* and *gold* and the long *i* sound as in *rind* and *wild*. Use each word in a sentence with your child.

Name _____

Pick a word from the box to finish each sentence.
Write it on the line.

answered brothers carry
different poor

_____

1. Rich or _____, a family could always have fun.

_____

2. When they _____ the knock at the door, people asked friends to stay for dinner.

_____

3. Dinner then was _____ because people cooked over an open flame.

_____

4. They had to _____ water from a well or stream.

_____

5. A boy and his _____ had to chop wood for the cooking fire.

Home Activity Your child learned to read the words *answered, brothers, carry, different,* and *poor.* Encourage your child to make up a story that uses these words and draw pictures to illustrate the story.

© Pearson Education 1

Name _____

Pick a word from the box to finish each sentence.
Write it on the line.

| answered | brothers | carry | different | poor |

_____
- - - - - - - - - - - - - - - - - -

1. Once there was a _____
   man living in Boston.

_____
- - - - - - - - - - - - - - - - - -

2. The man's _____ had just
   gotten off an amazing ship in the harbor.

_____
- - - - - - - - - - - - - - - - - -

3. He was surprised when he _____
   the knock on his door!

_____
- - - - - - - - - - - - - - - - - -

4. "If you will _____ the wood
   to the hearth, I will make you hasty pudding!"
   he told his brothers.

5. The men talked about the
   _____
   - - - - - - - - - - - - - - - - - -
   _____ inventions they had seen on their trip.

© Pearson Education 1

Home Activity Your child learned to read the words *amazing, answered, brothers, carry, different, harbor, hasty pudding, hearth, invention,* and *poor.* Invite your child to use some of these words to tell and act out the above story.

Name _____

Pick a word from the box to match each picture.
Write it on the line.

 p<u>aw</u>

 l<u>au</u>nch

| auto   draw   faucet   launch   saw   yawn |

1.

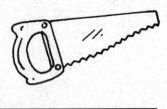

_____

_ _ _ _ _ _ _ _ _ _ _ _ _ _ _

2.

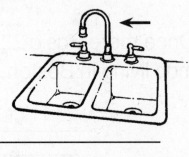

_____

_ _ _ _ _ _ _ _ _ _ _ _ _ _ _

3.

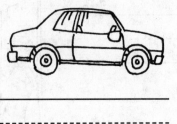

_____

_ _ _ _ _ _ _ _ _ _ _ _ _ _ _

4.

_____

_ _ _ _ _ _ _ _ _ _ _ _ _ _ _

5.

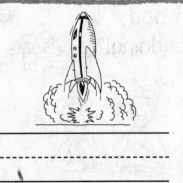

_____

_ _ _ _ _ _ _ _ _ _ _ _ _ _ _

6.

_____

_ _ _ _ _ _ _ _ _ _ _ _ _ _ _

© Pearson Education 1

 School + Home **Home Activity** Your child reviewed words with the vowels *aw* and *au* heard in *paw* and *launch*. Write each word above on a slip of paper. Have your child choose a word then give clues to its meaning for you to guess the word.

Name _____

Circle a word to finish each sentence.
Write it on the line.

br**ea**d

read   reed

_____

- -

1. Betsy _____ about a new flag.

thread   three

_____

- -

2. Betsy got out her needle and _____ .

spring   spread

_____

- -

3. Then she _____ out the cloth.

really   ready

_____

- -

4. Betsy was _____ to start.

head   hard

_____

- -

5. Now the flag hangs high above her _____ .

Home Activity Your child reviewed words with short e spelled ea as in bread. Have your child write the words bread, head, read, spread, and thread. Ask your child to write silly two-line rhymes using the words.

© Pearson Education 1

Name _____

Write the volume number of the encyclopedia you would use to find information about each topic.

Volume 1 A-B | Volume 2 C | Volume 3 D | Volume 4 E-F | Volume 5 G-H | Volume 6 I | Volume 7 J-K | Volume 8 L-M | Volume 9 N | Volume 10 O-P | Volume 11 Q-R | Volume 12 S | Volume 13 T | Volume 14 U-V | Volume 15 W-X-Y-Z

1. cheese _____   2. kites _____

3. Texas _____   4. mice _____

5. whales _____   6. baseball _____

7. vines _____   8. horses _____

9. zippers _____   10. apples _____

11. rain _____   12. lace _____

School + Home **Home Activity** Your child learned how to find information in an encyclopedia. Look through a children's encyclopedia with your child, making a game of finding new topics by using alphabetical order to find the right page.

Name _____

Computer Keyboard

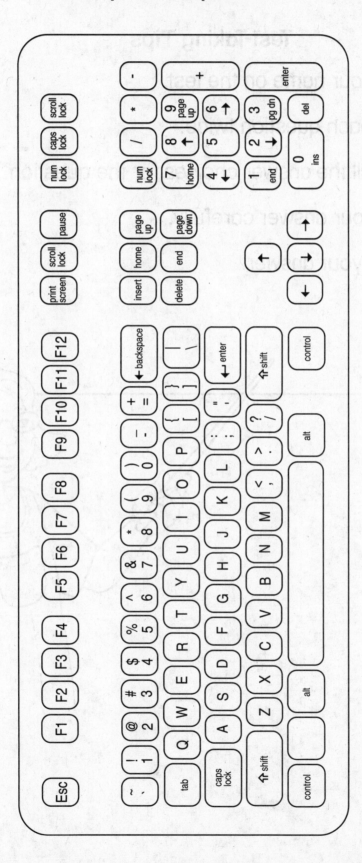

Test-Taking Tips

1. Write your name on the test.

2. Read each question twice.

3. Read all the answer choices for the question.

4. Mark your answer carefully.

5. Check your answer.

Name _____

Words I Can Now Read and Write

_____   _____
- - - - - - - - - - - - - - -   - - - - - - - - - - - - - - -
_____   _____
- - - - - - - - - - - - - - -   - - - - - - - - - - - - - - -
_____   _____
- - - - - - - - - - - - - - -   - - - - - - - - - - - - - - -
_____   _____
- - - - - - - - - - - - - - -   - - - - - - - - - - - - - - -
_____   _____
- - - - - - - - - - - - - - -   - - - - - - - - - - - - - - -
_____   _____
- - - - - - - - - - - - - - -   - - - - - - - - - - - - - - -
                                  _____
                                  - - - - - - - - - - - - - - -
                                  _____
                                  - - - - - - - - - - - - - - -
                                  _____
                                  - - - - - - - - - - - - - - -
                                  _____

I read _____

_____

_____

It was about

Words I Can Now Read and Write

Name _____

Words I Can Now Read and Write

_____   _____

- - - - - - - - - - - - - - -   - - - - - - - - - - - - - - -

_____   _____

- - - - - - - - - - - - - - -   - - - - - - - - - - - - - - -

_____   _____

- - - - - - - - - - - - - - -   - - - - - - - - - - - - - - -

_____   _____

- - - - - - - - - - - - - - -   - - - - - - - - - - - - - - -

_____   _____

- - - - - - - - - - - - - - -   - - - - - - - - - - - - - - -

_____   _____

- - - - - - - - - - - - - - -   - - - - - - - - - - - - - - -

_____   _____

- - - - - - - - - - - - - - -   - - - - - - - - - - - - - - -

_____   _____

- - - - - - - - - - - - - - -

_____

I read _____
_____
_____

It was about

Words I Can Now Read and Write

_____   _____

_____   _____

_____   _____

© Pearson Education 1

Name _____

Words I Can Now Read and Write

_____   _____
- - - - - - - - - - - - - -   - - - - - - - - - - - - - -
_____   _____
- - - - - - - - - - - - - -   - - - - - - - - - - - - - -
_____   _____
- - - - - - - - - - - - - -   - - - - - - - - - - - - - -
_____   _____
- - - - - - - - - - - - - -   - - - - - - - - - - - - - -
_____   _____
- - - - - - - - - - - - - -   - - - - - - - - - - - - - -
_____   _____
- - - - - - - - - - - - - -   - - - - - - - - - - - - - -
                                 _____
                                 - - - - - - - - - - - - - -
                                 _____
                                 - - - - - - - - - - - - - -
                                 _____

Name _____

I read _____

It was about

Words I Can Now Read and Write

_____   _____

_____   _____

© Pearson Education 1

Practice Book